JESUS
JOY

EXUBERANT

JESUS
JOY

My Painstaking Journey
To Deep Soul Winner's Joy

by
DAWID
MELEK

Jesus Joy
© Dawid Melek, 2019. First edition, November 2019

Published by Dawid Melek

Blogsites: dawidmelek.home.blog

ISBN: 9781706784654

Many names in this book have been changed. I tried my best to give credit where
due (due diligence, reasonable precautions, even though the book spans a lifetime),
and yet protect believers for the purpose of location nondisclosure, safeguarding
their privacy, identity and security, especially those in hostile, highly restricted
countries that are closed to the gospel, and where Christianity is illegal.

dedication

To our Heavenly Father, Jesus Christ, Holy Spirit, my immediate family in the heavenly presence of God (my first wife Nancy, Mother, Dad, brother Paul); my wife Barbie, daughter Angie, son Scott, daughter-in-law Niki, grandchildren Law, Maisy, Ezra, Feven, Ford, brother Pastor Bruce, sister Marilyn, all of my extended family, friends, including Chuck and Jeanene who led me and pointed me to Jesus, and brothers and sisters in Christ, with all of whom God placed me and from whom I have been greatly blessed. Exuberant "Jesus Joy" blessings and deep, sacred soul winner's joy to you with great thankfulness. And those unsaved of whom God allowed our paths to cross—may you one day be with us in His Holy Presence eternally.

about the cover

The inspiration for the cover began with the Cross/Heart Graphic displayed on the back cover of this book and prominently shown on the Gospel Handout. We decided to be more abstract with the design, while maintaining the key elements of the graphic. The heart, outlined with a soft brushstroke, was enlarged and goes beyond the borders of the page to represent that God's love is bigger than we can know and so much more than we can imagine.

Jesus commanded us to pick up our cross daily and follow Him. In a metaphorical sense, Dawid's burden to bring the gospel to those who are lost is represented through the image of him carrying his cross—a painstaking endeavor that shows his lifelong journey to fulfill his commission was a painful one. The highlight on the cross was designed to focus your attention where it always should be—on the cross.

The font used for the title was choosen because the letter "J" reminded me of a fishhook, which had me thinking of Jesus' statement that we would be fishers of men. The font for the subtitle was choosen to resemble handwriting to represent that this is Dawid's personal story and struggle to obey his Lord and Savior. We hope the design has accomplished our goal to represent this book.

Enjoy,
Frank Ballesteri

table of contents

acknowledgments

For those who helped me bring this book to fruition, directly and indirectly: Thank you Dear Heavenly Father, Jesus Christ, Holy Spirit, Missionaries, Martyrs, Evangelists, Pastors in the faith, and beloved precious family and friends whom God used to help forge the essence of my life, who helped make me laugh, cry, grow, prayed for me, helped me rejoice in the Lord, and of whom I am only able here to thank a small portion: Mother, Dad, Reverend Grandpa Johnston, Paul & Audrey, Marilyn, Bruce & Polly, Nancy, Scott, Angie, Barbie, Niki, Bonnie, Law, Maisy, Ezra, Feven, Ford, Ted & Edna, Carl, Evan & Collette, Uncle Lawrence & Aunt Mildred, Lois, Arnie & Diana, Don, Lori, Tim, Dennis & Linda, Jared & Mandy, Suneel, Jarrod & Laura, Gregg & Kenza, Joe & Sharon, Don & Laurie, Gary & Barby, Bob & Colleen, Dan & Julie, Larry & Julie, Steve & Cheryl, Doug and Sharon, Alan & Lynn, Ted & Rose, Carrie & Katie, Bryan & Chris, Lee & Margaret, Marge, Ron & Pat, Ric, Libbie, Craig & Allyson, Adam & Rachel, Charley & Nancy, Chuck & Jeanne, Bishara, Alex, Salim, Pat, Labib, Aaron, Doug, Mark, Don, Marty & Roe, Chuck & Pudge, Scott, Dave & Doris, Don & Cheryl, Rudy & Brenda, Jim & Betsy, Jennifer, Harold & Linda, Emory & Lizzy, Brad & Kathy, Dave & Laura, David & Carol, Robert & Carol, Bruce & Sandy, Chris & Wendy, Endashaw, Ross & Janet, Vernon, Bob & Mary Ann, Mack & Judy, Gary & Margie, Dave & Nancy, Ravi, Doug & Sheryl, Elton, Calvin & Trudy, Bill & Sandi, Barron & Donna, Ken & Barb, Todd & Billie, Kent & Diane, Tom & Ronna, Ken & Kaye, Dean & Val, Jim & Pam, Scott & Pam, Alison, Justin & Emily, Mel & Cindy, Bill & Diane, John & Linda, Jean, Robin & Lori, Glenn & Margaret, Adrian & Karen, Jim & Paula, Ron & Gaile, Missy, Ron & Dorothy, Al & Fran, Bill, Jim, Larry & Ann, Dave & Ruth, Gary & Candy, Brian & Becky, Atalla, Kent & Kelly, Sunny, Shahrukh, Rocio, Ron, Fred & Michelle, John, Ryan, Rev, Sully & Paula, Terry & Carole, Don & Christina, Marty & Joann, Brett & Lauren,

Hunter & Pat, Jay, Scott & Louise, Hal & Sally, John & Beth, Ahnna & Paul, Brad & Linda, Paul & Bonnie, Erik & Sueyuna, Eric & Alice, Salt, Robin & Anne, Ric, Joe & Jan, Chuck & Barb, Lori, Abiye & Aubrey, Horje & Marta, Kurian, Lorna, Lisa, Semse, Carter & Sheryl, Gordon & Daphne, Sukant & Seroja, Kevin & Cathy, Rashni, Ben & Jen, Judy, Lee & JJ, Seth & Linda, Dustin, Bob & Kelly, Greg & Sally, Hal & Sally, Setan and Randa, Joseph & Maria, Jack & Kim, Andy, Dustin, John & Kim, Hazel Anne, Sujani, Michael & Marny, Morgan Adams, Vennie & Orion, Debbie, Dave & Barb, Darron & Parker, Rich & Suzy, Rich & Becky, Greg & Raelynn, Roger & Sarah, Reggie, Mark & Robin, Paul & Sandy, Jim & Sheri, Ed & Sue, John & Ruth, Kerri, Theresa & Granna, Linda, Joe & Kate, Ruben & Kayla, Emmanuel & Kelly, Greg & Karen, Phil & Mariela, Richard & Elizabeth, Gary & Nancy, Austin, Andrew, Wade & Tracy, Bruce & Elsie, Michael, Aunty, Donnette, Victorious, Juvy, Amanda, Marc, Ernie & Martha, Christa, Cristy, Joshua, Jerry, Emily, Judy, Kevin & Debbie, Mike & Diane, Tony & Sarah, Randy, George, Cathy, Ray & Cindy, Jim & Silvia, Scott & Kay, Joe & Carol, Loy & Mary, Ron & Susan, Peter, John & Josie, Florence, Jerry, Bob & Mary Ellen, Paul & Judy, Mark & Linda, John & Donna, Ron & Glenda, Galen & Mary, Richard & Kathy, Bruce & Jill, Dave & Penny, Gary & Jeanne, Jim & Vicki, Jim & Debbie, Anthony and Patty, Jim & Mona, Howard, Brenda, Kevin, Shari, Roy & Vickie, Bruce & Elsie, Frank & Jacqueline, Aziz, Bob, Veronica, Darren & Parker, Sandy & Audie, Joel, Phil, Kim, Mark & Carolyn, Carol, Jim & Barb, John and Nancy, Alison, G. Paul & Ahnna, Paul, Wes & Gerti, Charlie, Jack, Jared, Bruce & Elsie, Lynn, and in appreciation and thanksgiving to all those whom I inadvertently or unintentionally overlooked or am unable to honor or recognize here, please forgive me as Christ has forgiven me.

With great thanksgiving, I express my eternal gratitude to Chuck and Jeanene King for sacrificially mentoring me and leading me to Christ in 1980. I am forever thankful for their unselfish obedience to Christ, along with their blessed friendship for over 40 years.

In memory of James Kent Hutcheson, PhD, I express my deep appreciation to his family. Kent and his wife, Diane, were the first to begin training me in evangelism over 30 years ago. This included Kent's publication, *Preparing And*

Sharing a Personal Testimony, along with a gospel handout. I prayed that God would allow me to publish *Jesus Joy* before Kent died, but that did not happen, which deeply saddened me. I wanted so much to be able to show him some good fruit that will last, which God bore through Kent's labor.

With deep appreciation, I thank author and editor Frank Ballesteri, who taught Bible study at work, for his unusual skill set assisting me with this book—help, healing, leading, guiding, counseling, encouraging, and never giving up on me as he spoke the truth in love. As he reviewed my manuscript, he wrote things like, "Keep writing,' 'Keep cleaning up,' 'Bring me into your story,' 'Tell me more,' 'Give me enough to take me along with you,' 'I need to know more,' 'Tell me how you feel about it,' 'Finish the conversation,' 'Tell the story,' 'How did it impact you?' 'Share more of the encounter,' 'Tell the rest of the story,' 'Paint a picture,' 'What did you learn from the experience?' 'Why are you so passionate about the story of the Gospel?" Our work together intensified as the book neared completion. I progressively recognized how wonderfully collaborative, fluid and dynamic our working relationship had become, as well as our friendship in Christ. I invited him on more than one occasion to co-write the book with me, which he politely declined. And I accumulated numerous nicknames for him, based upon humorous editing developments, including, "Oh-no,' 'Fishhook Frank,' and 'Baffles." This book would have exploded on the launch pad, had it not been for Frank's endless editing, cover design, layout, production for print and digital versions, plus blog development.

The people acknowledged above have soft hearts for God, great hearts. In like manner, in John Bunyan's book, *The Pilgrim's Progress*, there is a delightful character—a righteous soldier and protective pilgrim's guide, GREAT-HEART. Bunyan's account reminds me of a more modern version of the character GREAT-HEART. I love stories from the old wild West in the late 1800's and early 1900's, especially about the roots of cowboy ministry in Montana. Paul "Preacher Paul" Scholtz, tells about a young horseback circuit riding Preacher named William Wesley Van Orsdel—affectionately known by friends as "Brother Van." As an itinerant horseback evangelist and preaching missionary, Brother Van sent riders out in advance to help bring large gatherings to cabins where he was welcomed.

Cowboys, cavalrymen, freighters, and Native Americans became early converts of Brother Van. In fact, the Blackfoot's deep friend, artist and sculptor Charles M. Russell, my favorite Western artist, even did a watercolor painting entitled, *Brother Van Hunting Buffalo*, 1909. The Blackfoot Nation adopted Brother Van into their tribe and gave him the name "Great Heart," eventually calling him "Brother Great Heart." (Excerpts from *The Line Rider*, December 2010, p. 4)

With great love, appreciation and thanksgiving, it is the desire of my heart to honor God, thanking Him for creating my brother Bruce—Pastor, encourager, mentor, friend, confidant, and one of the greatest evangelists I have ever known. I am deeply grateful to be his brother. Had God not allowed me to be in the same biological family, I would never have written this book. Aside from prompting of the Holy Spirit, Bruce is the one God trained and used, inspiring me to be active in proclaiming my faith. Like Brother Van, I often refer to Bruce as "Brother Great Heart," particularly because I can never thank him enough for helping me envision God's amazing gift of "Jesus Joy," —that is, His deep, sacred soul winner's joy. As I share about how God equipped Bruce, and imputed many of His attributes and character into him, I trust you will agree that Bruce has a great heart for God, as he demonstrates year after year—and a heart for God desires to proclaim Jesus to the spiritually lost. And like Brother Van, my Brother Great Heart Bruce desires to see souls saved. I mentioned to him that our Bible study Pastor said from our study in Acts, "Wherever the Apostle Paul went there were riots." [Credit: Pastor Rudy Antle] So I humorously asked Bruce what happens wherever he goes. He responded, "I wanted you to know I make everybody happy—some by coming, some by leaving!" And on the subject of the Apostle Paul, I devote the following brief words to honor my other biological brother, Paul, in heaven, of whom Bruce, my sister Marilyn and I all greatly miss. Back to my brother Bruce—During the time of his pastoral ministry he used a number of evangelism strategies: D. James Kennedy's *Evangelism Explosion*, Billy Graham's *Steps to Peace with God*, Bill Fay's *Share Jesus Without Fear*, and Pastor Tom Elie's *One Minute Witness*. The following are a few of Bruce's quotes: "One time I told God, 'I don't know what I'm doing.' God's response to me was, 'You don't need to know what you're doing. You just need to know what

I'm doing!' 'One thing both believers and unbelievers have in common: They are all uncomfortable with evangelism.' 'The joy of obedience is clearly shown when we proclaim the gospel with someone to whom the Holy Spirit leads.' 'We have a Go Ye Gospel, but a Come Ye Church."

Introduction

I didn't expect my first wife to die of breast cancer. I didn't expect my second wife to suffer a brain stem stroke, become wheelchair bound, and struggle through three life-threatening colon surgeries, and that I would become her full-time caregiver. I didn't expect a crisis of faith at age 73. The greatest thing I didn't expect was that all my sins would be forgiven, granting me salvation in Christ, and eternal life—nor did I expect I could receive God's mercy and grace to help me in my time of need. I didn't know I could live without fear of failure, and that I could be secure in Jesus. I didn't expect God to grant me His peace, purpose, and power to stop sinning, so that my default tendency was to obey God and do what was right in His eyes instead of choosing sin. I didn't expect God to bless me with such wonderful family, friends, brothers and sisters in Christ. I didn't understand that our suffering can glorify God and lead to deeper hope and joy in Jesus. I didn't expect that God would allow me to serve His Holy Name halfway around the world, and to hang with the homeless and love the poor. I didn't expect to have living hope in God's living Word, Jesus Christ, and that He would give me the courage to be His disciple, deny myself, take up my cross daily, follow Him, and proclaim the gospel. I didn't expect to be so blessed—my Mother used to say, "I'm so blessed I can't handle 'em all!" Thank you, Lord, for giving me victory as an overcomer in Christ—freedom from the bondage of sin and death.

I didn't expect to write this book. Years after Jesus saved me from the death penalty of sin, I felt convicted to write, as God began to formulate in my heart and mind a book by the title of *One Man's WALK WITH GOD*. Decades later, God brought it to fruition as *Jesus Joy*. But how do I explain the joy? I can't, but God can. I hope I listened. I identified with the words, "Oh, how difficult it is to make anyone see and feel in music what we see and feel ourselves!" —Tchaikovsky, in a letter to his patron, Nadezhda von Mech, 1878. Only God can impute His work story through me, to you—His true story of my painstaking journey toward deep, sacred soul winner's joy. I trust as we synthesize evidence for proclaiming the gospel, we can agree that God bestowed exuberant *Jesus Joy* blessings upon us, as we encourage each other, together as partners in the gospel.

Have you ever known anyone whose career goal was to win a Nobel Prize for the world's top invention? Looking back on my earlier days, that seems like the epitome of selfish ambition. As I was reading the Bible in Church, Pastor Gary Wooley asked me, "What are you studying?" "I'm trying to learn how to have a pure heart," I responded. It is decades later, and I'm still learning. Another pastor told about when he was younger, "I thought I had fun, but I realized later that fun had me." [Paraphrased Credit: Pastor Jim Miller] I'm thankful for transparent pastors who helped me see the real Jesus, not an abstract, theoretical Jesus. Sometimes in their spiritual leadership, they "led with failure," which gave me hope in my own circumstances. Accepting Christ as my personal Savior was preceded by *discomfort*, because I had to die to self like a kernel of wheat falls to the ground and dies to produce many seeds. However, Jesus is the ultimate source of perfect *comfort*.

I am just a laborer sent forth into the harvest, an ordinary, lowly, weak, sin-prone normal, average, *lame vanilla* [Credit: Niki] Christian worker, not an ordained pastor, theologian, or even a skilled apologist for the faith, although I wish I was. I struggled taking Greek from a friend and audited Hermeneutics in Seminary. I am a child of God, brother in Christ, saint, a small part of a royal priesthood, and joyfully blessed of the Lord. My mission in writing this book is to proclaim God's exuberant "Jesus Joy" in my life, to bless, strengthen, encourage, unify and challenge the body of Christ to obey the imperative command of Jesus,

chapter 1
Dead-End Road

Life was good growing up as a farm boy—or so it seemed. At an early age I wondered why I was born, and asked myself, "What if I hadn't been?" If I had to pick the beginning of my painstaking journey toward exuberant Jesus joy—deep, sacred soul winner's joy, this would be it. But why the painstaking journey? For the first 35 years of my life, I had no relationship with God. I knew about God, but I did not truly know Him. I lived only for myself with neither purpose, direction, nor hope, oblivious to my spiritual condition, and yet God watched over me, protecting me from my own foolishness. I often made my morning plans on the farm, got the rifle and set out into the field with my favorite dog, Mike. I searched for pheasant, rabbit, squirrel, fox, whatever I could flush out.

While there was an abundance of chores on the farm, I always found time to get into trouble—like the time I thought it would be cool to use two trouser belts to climb a wooden pole in the barnyard, as a telephone line man would do. After I climbed several feet up on the pole, I slipped. The belt wrapped around my foot, strapping me to the pole, which left me hanging upside down, unable to extricate myself and with nobody to rescue me. Finally, my older brother heard my cries for help and arrived on the scene. For the first time ever, I was happy to see my brother until that wicked smile emerged on his face as he promptly took out some matches and lit them under my head, for entertainment! I was thankful when he finally let me down from my predicament—but conflicted with many mixed emotions.

Then there was the time I spotted an old car in a farmer's orchard, where it sat for years. I asked the farmer about the car, and whether it might be for sale, never asking when it had last been running! The farmer agreed to sell it to me for $15. So, my younger brother, along with a neighbor and I bought it and towed it home with a log chain, behind a tractor. We pulled the body off, leaving just the chassis. Then we began trying to figure out how we could get it running. In its bare-bones state, the chassis lacked such working parts as brakes, generator, lights and gear shift. As I welded a metal wheel at an angle to the frame for a seat, I didn't realize I was welding right by the gas line, and it caught fire. I extinguished the small flame, and then patched it up with electrical tape, which miraculously seemed to work—thankfully the fire didn't get near the gas fumes. In order to test the engine after completing our repairs, we had to park the chassis by the machine shed on top of the small hill and charge the battery each night. In the morning, we would adjust two handles I welded directly to the exposed transmission levers, to get the car into the correct gear, let it roll downhill, then "pop" the clutch which started the engine. After about two weeks of tinkering and tweaking the engine, we finally got it running. Then the fun really began as we tore through the gravel and mud farmyard, spinning the rear wheels which threw rocks everywhere. Because there were no brakes, the only way to stop the car was by jamming it into reverse and letting out the clutch. Then at dusk one evening, I decided to take it for a spin. So, I hopped in and started her up, never thinking of the consequences of my actions. I drove the bare chassis of what remained of the old car out onto the paved highway by the farm. I never realized just how loud the engine was, which alerted everyone on the farm of my exodus. Shortly after I arrived at a gravel road intersection about a mile from home, I was surprised to see my mother arrive in her car. She pointed the headlights on me in the darkness, so I would have a safer ride back to the house. I waited in tension for the perfect moment to make a run for it—I watched and waited for other cars coming, as well as being fearful that the highway patrol might show. I made a break for it. I went down the road at top speed with no helmet, leaving the safety of my mother's headlights far behind. Without headlights of my own, I overshot our home in the darkness. So, I downshifted for engine braking, to help slow the car. This revved up the engine, generating a huge fireball from the manifold, which produced just enough light to catch a glimpse of the neighbor's driveway. So, I quickly turned in, then backtracked home, surviving the episode—great evidence of God's mercy toward my stupidity. Eventually we dug a huge hole behind the machine shed and buried the chassis.

Fire was always a fascination for me—and a threat on the farm. There were corn crib fires, grain dryer fires, engine fires, self-started fires, and fires in fields. My Dad, brother and I set out one morning for a task on a small family farm near town. Dad wanted to burn a large pile of tree stumps and branches, which was a routine event. He started the fire with some kerosene, then left the project for my brother, Bruce, and I to finish. However, a strong wind developed, so much so that the fire soon raged and quickly turned into a firestorm. The fire roared as it accelerated. Branches snapped as they were consumed by the intense heat. It rapidly got out of control. As I walked between two fireballs, I realized my need to quickly escape. Bruce was shocked as he watched an old bird nest get vaporized in the flaming branches. When it disappeared in a puff of smoke, he knew we were both in serious trouble. The fire was not far from the town grain elevator, and dangerously close to huge pressurized anhydrous ammonia tanks. Soon there was the sound of a fire truck. But unfortunately, it could only approach us slowly, since it sunk into and out of deep furrows in the ground through the field. Once the fire was under control, there was the sheriff's inevitable question about why we were trying to burn down the town! I remember a deep struggle, convicted to do and say the right thing, help my Dad save face, but conflicted by my resentment toward him for putting us in this hazardous disaster zone! In all those moments, I had no idea or appreciation for how much God protected me from myself.

During that time of my life, I had little sense of personal identity, self-worth or credibility except through family, friends, sports, and my high school sweetheart and future wife, Nancy. While we dated, I always treasured looking forward to times driving together, with great anticipation of joy. Yet, my expectations were often accompanied by a feeling of mysterious emptiness in my spirit—there was something [or somebody] missing. Reality always seemed to fall short of my expectations. As wonderful as Nancy was, it was not possible for her to meet my deepest heart need, but at the time I didn't know that only God could. This emptiness spilled over into my college years, where I was often depressed, especially on Sunday nights, dreading another week of meaninglessness. I had no peace, purpose, or power to stop sinning (1 Corinthians 15:34). It was not like I never went to Church with my family—rarely did we miss. But I don't ever remember hearing a clear message of the gospel of Jesus Christ—probably because I wasn't listening.

Besetting sin took hold of my life. At an early age, the distinction between love and lust began to blur for me and plagued me throughout my life. It negatively affected many of my female relationships. I needed God's perfect love, but what I wanted and craved was lust. And this lustful attraction grew to include airplanes, flying, sports cars, racing, wealth, fame, and more. My mother prayed for my salvation for over 35 years. I was an example of what the Bible states in James 1:15, "Then, after desire has conceived, it gives birth to sin; and sin, when it is full-grown, gives birth to death." And death occurs at many levels and in many senses. For me, it started out as what some might call relatively innocuous sins. But Satan is clever. He is probably much more strategic than I give him credit. He led me down a many-year path of escalating sin, until it began to bring death—especially death of healthy, God-honoring relationships.

Together with some buddies from Church, Ric, Dirk, and Bob, I helped form our own alternative to Sunday School, something we called the Brat Club. We met in an obscure small room of the Church, which had a dirt floor, and we would plot our strategy under the light of candles. Many of my sins were not so much of omission, but of commission. I continuously broke God's law. James 2:10 states, "For whoever keeps the whole law and yet stumbles at just one point is guilty of breaking all of it." I had one thing in common with the Apostle Paul—I was like the chief sinner in 1 Timothy 1:14-16, "The grace of our Lord was poured out on me abundantly, along with the faith and love that are in Christ Jesus. Here is a trustworthy saying that deserves full acceptance: Christ Jesus came into the world to save sinners—of whom I am the worst. But for that very reason I was shown mercy so that in me, the worst of sinners, Christ Jesus might display His immense patience as an example for those who would believe in Him and receive eternal life."

I wanted to become a fighter pilot in the Air Force. So, after college I applied but was not accepted into officer training school, which kept me out of flight school. In order to avoid the draft and Vietnam war, I enlisted for four years. My primary duty in Europe was tracking Soviet military aircraft flights along what at that time was the East German border. Following military service, I worked in research and development for a medical company and was charged with the responsibility of generating new products and services. I developed my family, my career, my health, my aviation and financial goals around my own selfish ambitions. But these goals always left me empty. I had a false understanding of God and money. Looking at this chart, I never even considered setting spiritual goals, because I was spiritually blind and dead.

June 5 1978	MISSION AND PURPOSE: To gain control of all ability in order to influence others for good, through innovation. (Kurt Wright)				
	FAMILY	CAREER	AVIATION	HEALTH	FINANCIAL
'88 43	Prancer travel agency	Top World Innovator Top world invention Nobel prize	Top aviation Innovator Space flight EAA	AA10	I −$100,000 NW− 202,277 IP−11
'87 42			Fly around world EAA	AA9	90,000 175,893 10
'86 41			Sail ocean EAA		80,000 152,951 9
'85 40			Scott pilot's License EAA	AA7	70,000 133,000 8
'84 39	Family cruise		EAA	AA6	60,000 115,653 7
'83 38	Self-designed naturaliving solar home w/ G/h & AirS Observatory	Top U.S. Innovator Top U.S. Invention innomark ®	Soaring championship EAA	Climb mountain	50,000 100,567 6
'82 37	Family to Europe	garage Sales ~ Begin Now!	Fly to Paris Air show EAA	AA4 Lemans	40,000 87,450 5
'81 36	Sportscar	naturaliving SbI	Complete flt. ratings EAA Prancer pilot Lic.	Fly from Schoeman mountain	35,000 76,043 4
'80 35	Hawaii Mountain cabin	College Innovation course	Build powered sailplane	Racing	30,000 66,785

My mission, purpose and goals, June 5, 1978.

Because of my new product development work, I thought I was creative, and took a risk to become an independent new product consultant. I wanted to pridefully put up a sign on our garage door with the words, "I did it my way," like Frank Sinatra. I relished and thrived on such conceptual principles as the divergent/convergent creative process (quality of ideas as a function of quantity), as sketched here by a venture capitalist during a conversation together.

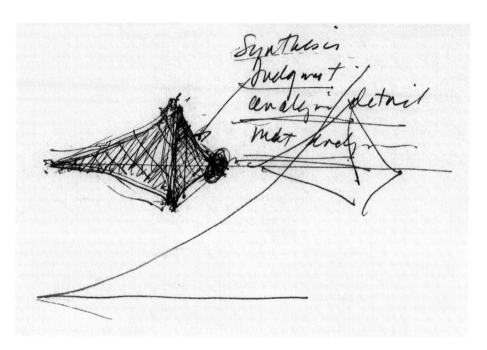

Divergent/convergent creative process sketch.

I learned that there was often a disconnect between the products and services companies offered, and what customers really wanted and needed. Often companies had to undergo major corporate cultural change to adapt, so they wouldn't get blindsided by competition. To help address this, I developed a creative seminar entitled, *After the Brain Storm Passes.*

As I tried to secure more clients as a new product consultant, I was speaking with a corporate Director of Research and Development, named Grant. I appealed to him for an opportunity to consult with his company, to help them generate new products. He said, "Dave, don't you realize big companies don't innovate?" My heart sank. I never forgot that shocking statement, because I suddenly realized

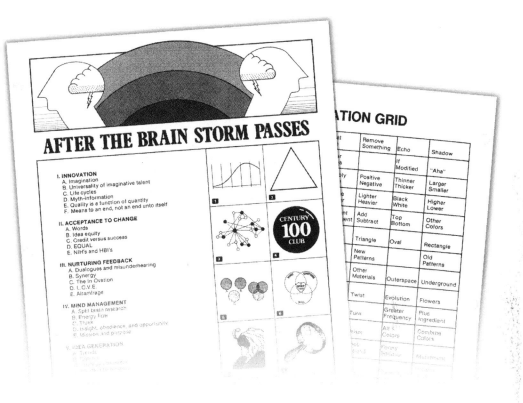

After the Brain Storm Passes creative seminar.

that the presupposition upon which I based my startup company was at risk of failure. I assumed that most companies would want the services of someone from outside, with considerable new product development experience, but I didn't understand the "not invented here" syndrome, and that many companies are risk averse! I also lacked professional sales skills, along with other essential skill sets.

Reality brought business pressure, stress and failure. I was angry at the world and this anger extended into my home where my marriage was about to collapse. Then neighborhood friends Chuck and Jeanene King invited our family to Church on Easter Sunday. Attending Church as a family gave me a feeling of comfort which I had not felt in years. God seemed to be drawing me to Himself and softening my hard heart. In retrospect, I realized I had many misconceptions about God. For example, I didn't think God cared about the details of my life, and I didn't know He could free me from worry. I began to seek God by reading the Bible which Chuck and Jeanene gave us. Because of my lofty, selfish goals, I started writing a book on creativity entitled *After the Brain Storm Passes*, based upon my seminar of the same name, because I thought I was so creative! But I was shocked when I read in Ecclesiastes 1:9 that "...there is nothing new under the sun," —I realized that man only discovers what God has created. I now understood that I could never finish the book without being accountable to God for who He was, what He had done, and what He did for me through Jesus Christ on the cross. I became convicted in my heart of my sin of independence and pride—C.S. Lewis calls this "spiritual cancer." Fellowship with God had not been possible because I was in denial, spiritually blind and dead, and I chose to go my own independent way, resulting in sin and defeat.

One of Satan's many lies to me was that my vocational career would end with no fulfillment and purpose. Thankfully, God granted and graced me with a deeply fulfilling career. I helped develop many new products and services, including copyright, trademark, and patent work. Then I realized I had the sin of *patent pride*, but God quickly humbled me! I received a "Special Inventor" award before I retired. I remember being surprised and so proud when I saw my name on the screen at a departmental meeting. About ten years later I thought I would check up on the status of the patent application. I was so excited to see the chronological events, until I read, "Application status is Withdrawn," and "Application status is Abandoned." It appears that several years before, similar patent applications were filed by competitors!

After the stress of losing my business, and almost losing my first wife, my 2-year old daughter Angie stuck the car key into a kitchen electric outlet and the sparks really flew—she wasn't hurt, but it sure was frightening! At that precise moment God "shocked" me into the conviction and realization that my life was going down a dead-end road—the consequence of my sin and idolatrous rebellion against God. The Bible states in Acts 5:31, "God exalted Him [Jesus] to His own right hand as Prince and Savior that He might bring Israel to repentance and forgive their sins." Instead of having freedom in Christ, I was imprisoned in spiritual bondage because of my sin. When I was young, my Dad spent a lot of time with the president of a bank near my hometown. He told me that the banker shed light on the plight of businesses up and down main street, stating that most of the business owners were bankrupt; they just didn't know it yet! In like manner, I was spiritually bankrupt; I just didn't know it.

After a two-year neighborhood Bible study with our friends Chuck and Jeanene, I accepted Jesus Christ as my Savior in 1980, a few months after our four-year-old son, Scott, received Christ. One of the hardest things I ever had to do was to call my mother and tell her that I accepted Jesus Christ as my Savior. This meant I was confessing to her that my rebellious path against God for over 35 years was a dead-end road—I had been going the wrong way. Even worse, I was spiritually blind and did not know it. I remember standing next to Chuck and Jeanene's car getting ready to join them for Church Sunday morning. I had a sense of peace and joy in my spirit which I never experienced before, the very thing I had been desperately seeking. Jesus transformed me into a new creation, according to 2 Corinthians. After I accepted Christ as my Savior, I wasn't perfectly sinless, but I had a strong desire in my heart to obey God, because He set eternity in my heart. I learned the hard way that the world promises much and yields little, but only Christ could satisfy my soul and assure me of eternal life. God continues sanctifying me, *little by little* (Deuteronomy 7:22). [Credit: Rev. Dr. Brad Strait] Even though I've read the Bible through several times and studied what it means to have a pure, broken, and contrite heart, I'm still learning and often fall short. As a "baby Christian," I had a dream of starting a Christian Flight Ranch to help young people. I wanted to build a log cabin, part of an idol of mine—mountains rich with game [Credit: Oswald Chambers], in the mountains and make it available for people who had two strikes against them in this world. [Obviously, God must have been working on my heart, since this goal was not entirely self-serving.] I found a beautiful lot in the mountains. I was about to make an offer on the land, but I sensed in my spirit God say to me inaudibly, "not now," or "not yet." God seemed to be teaching me the difference between "doing" and "being."

I still struggle with going down dead-end roads. If you asked me, I would be inclined to say "No," to the question, "Do you have an anger problem?" But the evidence tells a different story. Recently, I dropped the tray with my wife's dinner, spilling it all over the kitchen floor. My reaction was to throw the sharp knife onto the floor. I was so angry that the high quality, tempered steel knife shattered into two pieces. I picked up the handle and put it in the trash. However, I was unable to locate the sharp blade that was broken. I searched all over the floor, even using a flashlight, and concluded that it slipped into a crack under the counter and would be hard to recover. Later, I was shocked to discover the broken blade on top of the kitchen counter! That meant that it bounced back toward my face after it shattered. I thanked God several times for not allowing it to injure me, perhaps even putting out my eye. Lord, please help me have spiritual eyes to see when my life is headed down a dead-end road—have mercy on me so I can be Christ's disciple, deny myself, take up my cross daily, and follow Him. My prayer today is to glorify God's Holy Name and magnify His Holy Word.

chapter 2
Valley Of Grief

I didn't expect my first wife, Nancy, to die of breast cancer after 32 years of marriage, in 1999. She was a smart and gorgeous, tall blue-eyed blond who lived out the gospel. I called her "Prancer," a nickname given to her during our college years, by our close friend, Steve. Nancy became a great airline stewardess with a radiant, vivacious personality. Why she stuck with me, I will never know. Nancy underwent chemotherapy, radiation, and a stem cell transplant as she battled cancer, but nothing stopped the cancer from progressing. During home hospice as her final days came to an end, people came to bless her—and instead they left blessed by God through her. When Nancy closed her eyes for the last time, I began to walk the long, hard, and lonely road through the dark valley of grief.

> I walked the long, hard and lonely road through the dark valley of grief.

One Saturday afternoon after Nancy's death, I was rereading sympathy cards piling up on the kitchen table, something I should not have done in my grief. I quickly spiraled down into a frightening depression. Defeated and emotionally paralyzed, I was unable to stop crying for hours. In desperation and fear, I called my daughter Angie—then Barb Roberts, the Director of Caring Ministry at Church, who often visited us at home and the hospital. She referred to my tears as what Henri Nouwen called "flooding." In my emotional condition, prayer never occurred to me. That afternoon, Judy, a friend from Stephen

Ministry at Church, called to see how I was doing. I asked, "Why did you call?" She responded, "The Holy Spirit told me to." This was a critical act of God's grace at my most vulnerable time—without God's grace, I was without hope. Subsequently, I went through a grief support group at Church. After a couple of years, peers recognized my continued struggle with depression and suggested I seek professional counseling. This helped me as I came to reluctantly accept the sad, but realistic fact that the memory of losing Nancy would be with me the rest of my life. One day about six months after Nancy died, I came home from a birthday party, walked into our empty house and unexpectedly screamed, "God, why did you let her suffer so long?" This eruption of suppressed anger shocked me.

> I walked into our empty house and unexpectedly screamed, "God, why did you let her suffer so long?"

A friend asked me why I was always so positive before Nancy died. In all honesty, I always thought she would make it through. I was in complete denial. After 20 years I still wish the painful memories and tears would go away, so I could focus more on the joyful times, instead of grimacing in grief. But her physical death was not a loss to her. Prior to her death she coined the acronym, "C.H.R.I.S.T.," which meant, "Coming Home Really Isn't So Tough." Even though fear of death is the king of all fears [Credit: Pastor Craig Smith], Jesus gave Nancy victory over death, and she is gloriously in His presence. Hebrews 2:14 states, "Since the children have flesh and blood, He [Jesus] too shared in their humanity so that by His death He might break the power of him who holds the power of death—that is, the devil—and free those who all their lives were held in slavery by their fear of death."

I would not experience such deep grief again until 2010, when my second wife, Barbie, had a brain stem stroke. We met at Church through a mutual friend, Marge, who claimed she never did that sort of thing before! At that time, Barbie was a beautiful and bright architect, but the stroke left her with double vision, bouncy eyes, ataxia and no balance. She required brain surgery. Sitting in the waiting room during surgery, I started to dwell on the anger I experienced over all she lost as a result of the stroke. Although I called her "Barbie Doll," her friends from years before called her "Scripture Babe," because of her love for God and His Holy Word. And I often found myself asking, "Honey, help me understand this scripture." Fortunately, Barb Roberts was right there again with me in the hospital as she had been years before with Nancy—offering comfort and helping me understand the different mysterious stages of grief I was experiencing. Then in 2017, Barbie suffered through three life threatening colon surgeries. Even though she suffers every day in pain from the stroke, and would rather be in heaven, she prays for missionaries early every morning, and ministers to her caregivers. Although we all long for Barbie to be healed, she responds, "If I'm healed, my ministry goes away."

I'm so thankful for God's precious lovingkindness, and unfailing love (Psalm 36:7)—so loving, He desires that no one perish (2 Peter 3:9). Whether we are vibrantly alive, or even if we are facing death, God's mysterious love can always provide comfort. Perhaps in some mysterious way, God was preparing me to proclaim the gospel of peace, especially to encourage and help people see their need to be ready to answer to Christ before death calls. Because I have already faced tough questions, maybe God has emboldened me to ask others the tough questions in a truthful and loving way. For example, from 1 Kings 18:21, "How long will you waver between two opinions? If the Lord is God, follow Him . . ."

When I was very young, my sister, Marilyn, fell out of a tree when the branch she was on broke. She had the wind knocked out of her when she hit the ground. As she gasped for air, I begged her, "Please don't die." I didn't know any better, and she just laughed at me! Even Billy Graham says he tried everything he could to slow the aging process. In excerpts from his article *Death the Enemy* he stated, "We are living in a generation in which people try to forget death." "We try to cope with death by pretending it does not exist." "Young people have told me that they will not go to a funeral—they don't want even to think about death. They think, *everybody else is going to die, but I'm not. Someone else may have a motorcycle accident, but I won't.*" (December 2009 Decision Magazine)

I heard a pastor say once that most people die when they are not expecting it. Few, if any, expected the space shuttle Challenger's final minutes would end with the following transcript excerpts, which began two seconds after NASA's official version ended, with the words, "Uh-oh!" Times from the moment of takeoff are shown in minutes and seconds and are approximate. Out of respect for the flight crew, families and friends, names have been deleted.

T+ 2:29 "Our Father... (unintelligible)..."

T+2:42 "hallowed be Thy name... (unintelligible)."

T+2:58 "The Lord is my shepherd; I shall not want. He maketh me to lie down in green pastures... yea, though I walk through the valley of the shadow of death, I will fear no evil..."

T+3:15 to end None. Static, silence.

After I returned home from an overseas mission trip years ago, my wife and her caregiver started asking me questions. I broke down in tears and said, "I can't talk about it."

> I broke down in tears and said, "I can't talk about it."

Death was "just around the corner," at almost every turn, especially in heavily polluted air from cremation on "burning body day." In this country, horrific stories were a daily routine, such as the two young girls who were raped and hung from a tree.

There are places where, based solely on ethnicity, people are considered lower than animals. In just such a village, Bishop Camron's wife held the hand of a woman with a massive tumor, as she lay on a mat in the dirt, wreathing in pain, waiting to die. Our van was awkwardly silent as we slowly drove away on the bumpy dirt road. A day or two later, while praying for women evangelists in training, I was humbled, knowing that any one of them may face death for proclaiming their faith. And sadly, my roommate on this trip, John, died unexpectedly just before our next trip to return the following year—a hard loss for me and for our entire team. I treasured our 3:00 a.m. chats when neither of us could sleep. It was so painful, our Pastor warned people not to be his friend, because all of his friends die.

You don't have to go to a remote village overseas to find people in pain. One year I went on a trip to the mountains with my first wife, Nancy, and our daughter

Angie. We stayed in a lodge where a 7th grade boy lived with his grandparents, who managed the lodge. The boy and I started playing football in the snow, and it was fun—at first. Then the 7th grader started throwing the football hard at my stomach, even when I was only a few feet away, which hurt. So, I asked him to stop. I tried my best to stick with him—to relate to him. Eventually the boy began to share, "I used to live with my Mom. She was manager of an apartment. When she evicted a man, he stabbed her. She didn't die from that but she's dead now, and my Dad's a jerk." It was sad to hear his story. I tried to go to one of his football games in the mountains and stay in touch with him. I'm sorry to say it didn't work out, but I never forgot him. His story of grief gripped my heart, I think perhaps because God blessed me with a desire to see young people look to Jesus for the foundation of their life. They need more than just *empty motivation* [Credit: Pastor Paul Wolfe Smith]—they need the peace of Christ. I'm encouraged when I see youth sacrificially choose to follow Jesus. They need Him, they need Him now, because life is all too short as illustrated by excerpts of this story I read, "My 21-year-old son Chris was a pallbearer for the second time in six months this January. Another automobile accident. Another dead friend. Another opportunity to be confronted by issues of life and death, heaven and hell, faith and unbelief. This recent funeral was especially heart wrenching. It drew tremendous crowds of 'twenty-something' young people." "As the Church filled with college and high-school days friends, emotions ran high. Many of those who came were 'unchurched.'" "They... have limited exposure to (or affection for) church life. Orthodox Christian concepts of sin, atonement, judgement, and salvation are largely unfamiliar and disinteresting to them. But nothing gets our attention like death. The pain and confusion I saw on those faces broke my heart. They looked '...harassed and helpless, like sheep without a shepherd.' (Matthew 9:36) Here was a life changing moment for ministry!" "Who makes up this group of people? What makes them such a distinct harvest field? How do they think? How can we reach out to them...?" "The Good Shepherd bids us, through Him, to seek and to save what was lost." (Editor, Evangelical Presbyterian Church *Reflections* Magazine, Spring 1998)

I've experienced the evilness of death, so I appreciate author Ian Barclay when he wrote the following excerpts, "One word the Bible uses for death is *exodus*, which means 'the way out.'" "My first wife died after battling with cancer for nine years. As an Anglican clergyman, I had often tried to help other people in their loss and had performed hundreds of funeral services, but it wasn't until Sheila's death that I understood something of the trauma involved. Those who suffer this way are called 'bereaved,' coming from the word reave, meaning 'to ravage, rob and leave desolate.'" (*Death and the Life After*, p. 10)

One Summer Barbie and I served as counselors at a rodeo Bible camp. It broke my heart when I learned one of the kids said she didn't need to pray because her Dad says that God is dead. Jim Chamley, a cowboy preacher, stated, "You might be rough and tough on the surface, but if you aren't just a little bit scared deep down, you are probably nuts. You need to give your life to the Lord because you never know when it might be your last ride." Sadly, proving his point, a professional bull rider died recently from injuries suffered during a national stock show and rodeo in our city. When that young man prepared to ride, he probably never suspected it would be his last. I wonder if he was saved, did someone take the time to share the gospel with him?

At a custom car show, I saw a lady I had seen at a previous automotive event. She was displaying a memorial "show car" to commemorate her son who died. I felt uncomfortable and did not know what to say or do, so I took her non-profit business card. Later I asked my brother Pastor Bruce, what I should do. He spoke conceptually about her "redeeming the tragedy." So, in trying to encourage her, I mailed her a letter, along with God's Word in a gospel handout, thanking her for trying to redeem the tragedy, and extending my condolences. I trust on faith that God will bring good out of her tragic loss. The Bible states, "The last enemy to be destroyed is death." (1 Corinthians 15:26) But we can be encouraged in Christ, as the Apostle Paul wrote, "Brothers and sisters, we do not want you to be uninformed about those who sleep in death, so that you do not grieve like the rest of mankind, who have no hope." (1 Thessalonians 4:13)

My heart broke, in a flood of tears repeatedly, while twice reading Emily Foreman's book *We Died Before We Came Here*, as she documented her family's call to sacrifice—serving on the front lines, the tip of the spear, bringing the gospel to a nation where Christianity was illegal. Sadly, her husband was murdered by extremists. Upon her return to the same mission field over a year later, she said, "I felt the weight of loss like an anvil on my heart, yet it was mixed with indescribable joy and peace." (pp. 173, 174) Emily stated, "But Stephen didn't lose his life. He found it." The Bible helped me better understand her profound insights, when I read, "One person gives freely, yet gains even more; another withholds unduly, but comes to poverty." (Proverbs 11:24) In a different and very limited sense, when witnessing for Christ, I often expect nothing in return—yet receive everything.

chapter 3
Living Hope

In the 1990's, Helen, a caring ministry friend and woman of faith with Stephen Ministries, gave a blessed devotion about living hope from 1 Peter 1:3, which had a lasting impact on me. Many years later, I got excited when I read a reference to Jesus as the living Word in 1 Peter 1:23. To paraphrase, the evidence is clear from God's Word that we have a living hope in God's living Word, Jesus Christ. He offers us true hope, not the false hope the world offers. The book *PAUL Apostle of the Heart Set Free*, p. 113, sheds light on the magnitude and infinite majesty of Jesus. Author F.F. Bruce speaks of the empty tomb and resurrection appearances marking the transition from the historical Jesus to the exalted Christ. Thankfully, Christ's love set my heart free, transforming me with the joy of living hope in Him—God's *promise of righteous glorification* (Galatians 5—paraphrased). [Credit: Pastor Timothy Keller and Marc Ragusin]

A few years after my salvation in Christ, God placed a desire in my heart to be active in proclaiming my faith. During the 1980s, I had a beautiful, large wooden table with a glass top I used as my desk in the basement of our home. God began mysteriously leading me to research and study over 200 gospel handouts, which I would spread out on this desk. Gathering them from every source available, I searched for months for the common threads running through them. It seemed like a collection I was building, but it soon became clear that God was leading me toward a specific purpose—to consolidate His Word into a gospel message I was to proclaim to the spiritually lost. This process of developing a gospel handout seemed to begin when I had a custom-made white sweatshirt printed for my mother, who was a great woman of God and His Word. The sweatshirt featured a graphic in the shape of a heart made from a thorn bush, symbolizing the Biblical crown of thorns on Christ's head. Then the words "Jesus Loves You" appeared prominently.

Initial sweatshirt for my mother, leading to the gospel handout.

In October, 1995 I started work on the first draft of the gospel handout. I envisioned a red die-cut, heart-shaped pamphlet, with the words, "Jesus Loves You" on the cover. On the inside, I combined Bible scripture and some of my own words. But it would have been impractical and prohibitively expensive to produce. Then I roughed out a crude graphic of a bullet hole, which symbolized the spiritual "hole in our heart" that only God can fill. This represented God setting eternity in the hearts of men (Ecclesiastes 3:11). I wrote such elementary, uninspired human words as, "...You have a problem, however, because like the moon, your heart has a dark side." "...Jesus Christ loves you. He is good news because He offers you a new chance, a new day, a new love, and a new life. He wants to fill the hole in your life and replace the hurt in your life." "...Embrace Him like a drowning person grabs a rescuer who has come to save him."

I sketched rough graphics for the cover of the first production gospel handout for some period of time, using a combination of heart and cross symbols. I

Red heart and cross gospel handout graphic.

never got it to where I thought it was quite right! Then one beautiful, sun-shiny Saturday morning at the dining room table, I was sketching, when God gave me a vision of a red heart and cross graphic. My friend, Paul Galloway, a professional artist, rendered it for me and successfully captured the power behind the symbol.

Much like music, images can be powerful and transcend normal language barriers. Pastor Dave Strunk stated, "Music—the international language of the soul—touches and engages our heart so our mind can understand." In like manner, the symbolic cross of Christ and the heart are universally understood throughout much of the world. I've discovered over many years that there is almost instant recognition by both believers and unbelievers throughout many countries of the world—when they see the heart and cross graphic, they know

I am proclaiming the good news about Jesus, and that the heart is involved. Additionally, the color red correlates with the shed blood of Christ for our sins, and white often symbolizes the purity of Jesus. Soon the first gospel handout was born with the above-mentioned graphic representing what I called "Sin of man" [heart] — "God's salvation plan [cross]." One day while on the bus, a wonderful lady and follower of Jesus pondered the graphic and then commented, "Love and the cross are one and the same." The full printed gospel handout is also online. Additionally, the red heart and cross stand-alone graphic is online, to help communicate and reinforce the good news of Jesus through visual imagery, even without the words!

Besides the heart and cross graphic on the cover, the first production gospel handout included the words, "There is Good News for you!" It was printed in a quantity of 5,000, and included scripture passages, along with many of my own words. It showed illustrations of the "hole in our heart," which still makes me laugh. The funny thing was that the artist's rendition, at my direction, looked exactly like a bullet hole! At the time, it seemed appropriate, but in retrospect I am still shocked that I published it. Thankfully, it is not beyond God to use my misjudgment. While in the car with my mother on the way to meet a friend and her grandson, I had the new gospel handout with me. During the drive, we talked about our visit with young Kenny and his Grandmother. That gospel handout somehow ended up in Kenny's hands. Sometime later I received a letter, which read, "Dear David [,] My name is Kenny Wilson III [.] I am 6 years old [.] I read the track you made the hole in the cross [heart] and I asked Jesus to come in my heart [.] Thank you [,] Kenny III" This was a great blessing and encouragement to me from God. After many years, I tried to connect with Kenny, but with no success. He remains in my prayers.

Early on, I produced a low quantity of bumper stickers, using the red heart and cross graphic. There is nothing like a Jesus Loves You bumper sticker to help change your driving habits! I still use a bumper sticker that was given to me by our friend Colleen. It states in large letters, *Christ Died for our Sins*, from I Corinthians 15:1-4. I trust in the power of God's Word to bring conviction, especially to help unbelievers begin to grasp their sin, before they can understand

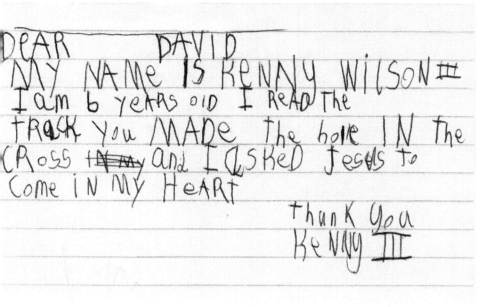

DeAR   DAVID
MY NAMe IS KeNNY WILSON III
I am 6 yeARs old I ReAD The
tRack You MADe the hole IN the
CRoss they and I asKed Jesus to
Come iN MY HeARt
                              thunK You
                              KeNNY III

Letter received from Kenny regarding the gospel handout
and "Hole in the Heart."

why they need to be saved. I pray for every driver directly behind me when I am stationary in traffic, especially when they pull up close to the back of my car. I'm never sure what reaction I will get from the person slowly passing me after viewing my bumper sticker. A Christian bumper sticker may be offensive to some, and there are times I can feel their resentment. One time I suddenly realized a woman pulled up closely behind my car, then started honking at me, followed by her female passenger screaming at me out her side window. Over the years, I have been waved at with numerous obscene gesticulations, laughed at and frowned upon. I've often wondered if someone was going to hit me as they pulled up close to the back of my car, then rapidly swerved out, maneuvering their car close to mine, and then swerved their car just inches away from my front bumper as they dart back into my lane. Then there are those times when other believers are encouraged and thankful when they see a spiritual bumper sticker or fish symbol on my car, as I am blessed when I see them on other's cars. Together we proclaim God's Word with boldness (Book of Acts).

One day God strongly convicted me to make the second iteration gospel handout contain "Scripture alone," with none of my own uninspired human words that always ended up disappointing me. It was to be God's Word alone, which never disappoints. This was very freeing to me because whenever I used my own "clever" phrases, they always ended up falling short, and led to frustration and bondage. I was in bondage because I trusted in my own words—words that did not preach the gospel. Whenever I thought I had just the right words of my own, I would think of other words that might be better, then the cycle of despair would start over again. Only God's Holy Word truly points us to His grace—our only hope to repent of our sins and be saved, denying ourselves and taking up our cross daily to follow Jesus. Once I made the final decisions on the choice of Scripture only, I was overwhelmed with the conviction that I was accountable to God.

The second gospel handout was produced in a quantity of 25,000, at about 4.5 cents each, and lasted several years, until 2015. With the help of a team of about ten, including being led by our Heavenly Father, Christ Jesus, and Holy Spirit, we updated to the third iteration and printed 50,000. We dropped one heart and cross graphic and reduced the number of verses, which allowed us to cut down the size of the handout from 6-panel/two-fold to 4-panel/single fold. This reduced the unit cost to 2.9 cents each.

Lost souls are worth every penny. It's the best investment I've ever made, with an eternal return on investment! Proverbs 3:13-15 states, "Blessed are those who find wisdom, those who gain understanding, for she is more profitable than silver and yields better returns than gold. She is more precious than rubies; nothing you desire can compare with her." Why wouldn't anyone want to make a small investment to help proclaim the gospel, that may lead to another's salvation? As one persecuted evangelist stated, "If we save one woman or one man, it will be worth it." (*The Voice of the Martyrs* (VOM), May 2019, p. 8, 9) Over a period of about 40 years, I can count on the fingers of one hand, the number of people who received Christ as I spoke with them—but those few have eternal worth.

The printer voluntarily put the gospel handout on a 6-color press and added an aqueous coating at no extra cost, an unexpected gift from God, to protect the

Genesis 1:1 In the beginning God created the heavens and the earth.

Genesis 1:26 Then God said, "Let us make mankind in our image,"

Genesis 6:5 The Lord saw how great the wickedness of the human race had become on the earth, and that every inclination of the thoughts of the human heart was only evil all the time.

Psalm 53:1 The fool says in his heart, "There is no God." They are corrupt, and their ways are vile; there is no one who does good.

...and all are justified freely by his grace through the redemption that came by Christ Jesus.

Romans 6:23 For the wages of sin is death, but the gift of God is eternal life in Christ Jesus our Lord.

I John 1:8-9 If we claim to be without sin, we deceive ourselves and the truth is not in us. If we confess our sins, he is faithful and just and will forgive us our sins and purify us from all unrighteousness.

Galatians 5:19-21 The acts of the flesh are obvious: sexual immorality, impurity and debauchery; idolatry and witchcraft; hatred, discord, jealousy, fits of rage, selfish ambition, dissensions, factions and envy; drunkenness, orgies, and the like. I warn you, as I did before, that those who live like this will not inherit the kingdom of God.

Matthew 1:21-23 She will give birth to a son, and you are to give him the name Jesus, because he will save his people from their sins." All this took place to fulfill what the Lord had said through the prophet: "The virgin will conceive and give birth to a son, and they will call him Immanuel" (which means "God with us").

John 10:30 "I and the Father are one."

Matthew 5:17, 21-22 "Do not think that I have come to abolish the Law or the Prophets; I have not come to abolish them but to fulfill them. "You have heard that it was said to the people long ago, 'You shall not murder, and anyone who murders will be subject to judgment.' But I tell you that anyone who is angry with a brother or sister will be subject to judgment.

Third iteration gospel handout, showing the red heart and cross graphic.

blood red color and make it "bounce." God has been doing a miraculous new thing that has borne lasting fruit through this walk of faith. During the Christmas season, I have enjoyed adding a gospel handout to a box of peppermint tea, showing red and white peppermint candy on the cover. People appreciate it when I tell them the red represents the blood of Jesus shed for them, and the white represents the purity of Christ, whose body was broken for them. Some people have used candy canes to illustrate the same message. If you ask the Holy Spirit to guide you, counsel you, and help you proclaim the gospel—you will be amazed at what He can accomplish through you!

God can use gospel handouts in an infinite number of ways to draw people to Himself. Even though a gospel handout is just one spiritual tool, it can powerfully present God's gift of salvation as a tangible, tactile, leave behind free gift. For example, in addition to giving gospel handouts directly to people as good news gifts of "Jesus Joy," God convicted me to insert them into magazines, especially when waiting in medical offices. Sometimes this painstaking work can be somewhat tension filled, trying to quickly and discreetly insert gospel handouts into dozens of magazines, not knowing who is watching either in person or on camera. When I become anxious, I just trust God is working through me. In the case of my dentist, his staff graciously allows me to keep gospel pamphlets inserted into their extensive magazine assortment available on the waiting room table—and my nutritionist makes them available for her clients. Whenever I go into almost any store, building or office, I try to prepare myself to make the mission of proclaiming the gospel my highest priority. Usually this comes in the form of passing a gospel handout to a person God shows me—as He opens a door of ministry. These blessed spiritual encounters frequently result in unexpectedly meeting or conversing with someone. Additionally, I leave gospel handouts anywhere and everywhere as *love drops—faith drops.*

> I leave gospel handouts anywhere and everywhere as love drops—faith drops.

Sometimes when entering a store or office, I go straight to the men's restroom and place a few gospel handouts. One day in a restroom a man initiated a conversation with me. Even though he was very friendly as he spoke, he uttered a barrage of vulgar words. We briefly conversed, I listened, then as we left the restroom, I introduced myself and he said his name was Robert. I asked him if I could give him some good news. He looked at the gospel handout briefly, then kindly received it. Then I prayed for his salvation as we parted.

God often shows me new avenues to proclaim the gospel I never thought of before. People need the gospel and the hope it brings through God's living Word, Jesus Christ, according to 1 Peter 1:3, 23. Occasionally I have cut out the red heart and cross graphic from the gospel handout, and pasted it onto greeting cards. My goal was to encourage people with attention getting visual good news, while tailoring the card to each individual. I provided the red heart and cross graphic on the back cover of this book for anyone to copy and use in their evangelical ministry. Since God gave it to me, it is only fitting that I share it. I pray according to 2 Timothy 1:7, "Holy Spirit, help me not be timid, but give me power, love, and self-discipline." God provides all of us the opportunity to proclaim Christ through extended conversations and relationships with unbelievers. Opportunities abound, even in brief encounters with people who are desperately searching for true, loving relationships, struggling with life, and without hope—and with no anchor for their soul. He commands us to be active in proclaiming our faith (Matthew 28:19, Mark 16:15, Isaiah 12:4, et. al.). In 2 Timothy 4:5, we are told to do the work of an evangelist. Hopefully, printed gospel handouts and electronic gospel messages serve as useful spiritual tools to help us obey God. May we flood the world with the gospel light of our lives, leading many to righteousness (Daniel 12:3). Historically, gospel handouts were used by John Bunyan (author of The Pilgrim's Progress) in the 1600s; Charles Spurgeon (English Baptist pastor, preacher, educator) in the 1800s; evangelist Bill Bright, and Billy Graham, who stated, "Nothing surpasses a tract for sowing the seed of the good news."

God seems to use me most often as a "sower" of the gospel (1 Corinthians 3). Christ's salvation is simple, yet profound. Scripture makes clear that we need to confess our sin and repent—the Greek word for repent, *metanoeo*, is equal to the military command "about face." It is a change of mind that causes a change in direction. God is perfect. He never lies, and He has stored up goodness for us according to Psalm 31:19. Jesus Christ offers us eternal rest and eternal peace for our soul, even as a hostile world rages in chaos, exchanging our sin for Christ's righteousness. While speaking with a man at a pancake house, I asked him, "How do you explain the chaos in the world?" "I can't," he answered, even though he had a clearly delineated philosophy of how the world works, especially since he was rather financially prosperous. We spoke for just a few more minutes. He was nice enough to receive a gospel handout. I thought he was kind, just to have a brief spiritual conversation with me. As he parted, I was thankful God allowed me to talk with him. I immediately prayed for his salvation and continue to do so.

Early in my life, I thought Christianity was a crutch—but I was spiritually crippled, blind and dead in my sin—I needed Christ. In Matthew 7:13, 14, Jesus said that few will find eternal life. This is a frightening truth. Many will be doomed to eternal condemnation in the lake of fiery hell due to their lack of faith. But by God's great grace, the gospel can save them. We all need to satisfy our soul (Isaiah 58:11), and receive eternity that God set in our hearts (Ecclesiastes 3:11).

Years ago, I was blessed by God through a friend at work, Elton, to learn about Arthur Blessitt, who carried a wooden cross around the world. In Luke 9:23 Jesus stated in part, "... "Whoever wants to be My disciple must deny themselves and take up their cross daily and follow Me," so God sends us, leads us, appoints and anoints us in our different callings. Documentaries and books about Arthur Blessitt carrying the cross inspired me. The Holy Spirit led me years later to build a large wooden cross and carry it on the street, but only once! My faithful friend, Charley Cook, who once told me, "Remember Jesus," helped me build the cross, along with the curiosity and help of a sweet young neighborhood girl who just showed up. Both were great blessings to me. We added a built-in wheel

Building the cross with the help of my faithful friend, Charley Cook.

at the bottom so the heavy weight of the 8-foot high cross wouldn't drag on the cement.

Finally, the cross was complete and ready to carry on the street. Unfortunately, I soon realized I didn't have enough courage to go out with it. I had to pray on my knees in the house for an hour and a half before I could head out. As I initially walked down the sidewalk, the afternoon sun cast my shadow on the grass, and when I saw it, I sensed God say inaudibly to me, "Dave, this is as much for your benefit as it is for anyone else." I was deeply Humbled! While carrying the cross, I saw a man sitting on a chair in a driveway. He was visiting his son and claimed to be an elder in a Christian Church in a different country. I asked him, "Do you believe you can know that you will have eternal life?" He responded, "Fifty-fifty chance." Yet the Bible clearly stated that we can know (1 John 5:10-13). I was stunned, and sadly disappointed at his response. As I walked further, a lady on the street told me how I could pray for her. Then I approached another man working on the engine of his Corvette in his driveway. When he spotted me carrying the cross, he quickly ducked down behind his car! In this same area near my home on a day when I was not carrying the cross, I gave a gospel handout to a young girl and told her that Jesus loved her very much. She said, "Thank you—that's good to know."

Decades ago, at an event in a park, a man silently stood, reading the Bible to himself. Just looking at his face, I sensed a Holy boldness in him, which inspired me. I don't even know if I was saved at that time. And a missionary friend of mine, Dave, and his wife Susan were once on a three-hour bus ride in a distant land, when a lady got on the bus and began preaching the gospel. Dave stated, "What a testimony. She reminded me of John Wesley who rode thousands upon thousands of miles preaching the gospel from the back of his horse. May we be as faithful."

chapter 4
Brief Encounters

Since I am not a theologian, in most cases the daily opportunities God opens for me to proclaim the gospel sometimes seem like ships passing in the night. It might be a chance encounter in a parking lot, by a cash register in a store, on the hiking trail, or an infinite number of ways in which God orchestrates my life moment by moment. I found that people seem to love having someone take an interest in them. Frequently I ask people, "Where did you grow up?" This often bears good fruit. God continues to bless me, as I watch Him work through politely engaged conversation with people in these brief encounters. These short moments, when conducted in sincere love, can multiply our joy and make a huge difference for Christ—e.g., the thief on the cross and Nicodemus! The average length of Jesus' conversations as recorded in the Gospels, was 42 seconds long, according to author Carl Medearis. And, even if I never see a person again, I often continue to pray for them for years. "Jesus often approached strangers... like the woman at the well, Zacchaeus who was in the tree, and Matthew the tax collector. Other times Jesus built relationships..." [Credit: Tom Elie, *One Minute Witness*]

One day I found myself walking alongside a young man in a grocery store named Keon, so I offered him a gospel handout. I asked him, "Are we brothers in Christ?" He smiled and said, "Not yet. My wife is a believer, but I'm not." At that moment, I sensed in my spirit God was doing something mysteriously special in this man's heart, because Keon started asking me several deep spiritual questions. "What about all those other religions?" "Is Jesus the only way?" How long have you been saved?" I briefly gave my testimony proclaiming faith in Christ. When Keon seemed satisfied with my answers and my story, I asked him if he would share about our "chance" meeting, our conversation and the gospel handout with his wife, to which he agreed. I told Keon that he knew about the power of God since he just witnessed Him create an instant bond of spiritual friendship between us. We both parted joyfully.

On Resurrection Sunday, Easter 2016, I said to God, "40,000 tracts remain Lord. What do I do?" Since that time God greatly accelerated the number of people receiving good news through the gospel handout. Hopefully God is being glorified through this. These brief encounters remind me how much God is at work through His servants. In the hardware store, Peter received God's Holy Word through a gospel handout with a big smile and said, "Pennies from heaven! I will read it on my lunch." And shortly after, a man named Cory received the gospel handout and said, "I will read it." As I waited in line to return something at another store, I lacked faith, believing that it was not possible to give the gospel handout to the lady in front of me. Suddenly she turned around and said, "I would be remiss if I didn't share my business card with you." "I would be remiss if I didn't share mine with you," I said. She kindly received the gospel handout. And when Eric, another gentleman I met, received the Bible scripture, I was delighted as he said, "Thank you. I could always use a little uplift." Then another man named Ricky said after receiving the gospel handout, "It's nice to be blessed for a day." But Erin at the bank didn't say a thing when she received the gospel handout—she just smiled radiantly, and her eyes lit up! I was filled with "Jesus Joy" for the whole day! I once asked a young pastor how I could pray for him. He said, "Breaking free." I offered a gospel handout to him and told him I would be happy to provide any quantity the Church would like. He did not take me up on my offer.

On another occasion, I just entered the hiking trail, when an elderly lady named Nancy was walking with some difficulty. She was kind enough to receive the gospel handout with God's Word and responded, "That's very kind of you." God continued to bestow His stored-up goodness upon me (Psalm 31:19), when I crossed paths with a longtime friend, Maynard, a financial guy. I found Maynard to be spiritually strong in his walk with Christ. He had a wonderful way with people and seemed to know exactly how to connect and point them to Jesus. He often found that a recent devotional seemed a natural fit for what someone was going through in their life. On this occasion, Maynard mentioned a longtime friend, Jerry, to whom he often witnessed, who was experiencing serious family health issues. Maynard hoped he might be an encouragement through an appropriate devotional message. We continue to pray for Jerry. As God kept opening doors of ministry, He seemed to progressively increase my joy throughout the day.

One evening I was walking on the trail near our home. It was picturesque along the path with the only light coming from the surrounding homes and the city, reflecting off low level snow clouds. That is when a young man walking with a small dog approached. I asked, "Ready for the snow?" Not expecting much of a response, he asked how much snow was forecast. "How long ya been out here?" I asked. "Since Oh-one," he responded as we struck up a conversation. He said his name was Brad. I told him I was just an old guy and how many years before God gave me the red heart and cross graphic on the gospel handout, which he received with interest. As we parted, Brad said, "Thanks for the scripture, Dave!" I prayed that God would save him, redeem him, choose him, and rescue him.

God often surprises me with brief encounters—and yet it is always a blessing when He extends my time with someone. God convicted me to evangelize at a presidential nominating convention, to adopt its national platform and officially nominate candidates for President and Vice President. I felt a little uncomfortable at the light rail station as I prepared to depart, because I rarely took light rail. I was unsure of exactly how self-ticketing worked using the machine dispenser. As I stood by the train, I noticed the engineer's head was sort of half sticking out the window. I greeted him and asked him a question about ticketing. God allowed me to quickly offer a gospel handout to him, which he was gracious enough to receive. I boarded the train and contemplated what I thought was a clear vision of how I would reach out with the gospel when I arrived downtown, not knowing God had a different plan. Within moments of the train departing, I struck up a conversation with a young drug addict. We talked for a while about himself and spiritual matters and by the time he got off at his destination he willingly received a gospel handout. At the convention, I was quickly indoctrinated about the "Red Line," or "Red Zone," with multiple automatic weapons to help me understand the area beyond which I was not to enter. God allowed me many interesting, challenging, and unusual opportunities to proclaim the life-vital message of Jesus Christ with scores of people that day, mostly using gospel handouts. A few people were even interested in listening!

One day I was at the dentist, because I had two teeth that needed a root canal. The endodontist felt bad because she had to inject me multiple times before the anesthesia would take effect. It was one of my worst experiences in a dental chair. Following the procedure, when she walked away, I asked her if I would see her in heaven. She said, "I hope so. I sure hope so." Unfortunately, I was not in a position to proclaim the gospel, so I left a gospel handout for her with the assistant. I hope she received it.

Whether brief encounters or long-lasting relationships, I am reminded of when I heard a pastor pray the words, "relational ministry of Jesus." These words had a powerful impact on me, probably because of God's covenant love relationship with believers. God pursued a relationship with us, and to reflect that we, in turn, should build relationships with others. This notion of the relational ministry of Jesus profoundly altered the course of my life, as it relates to my own identity in Christ. This is crucial, when proclaiming the gospel. Understanding who I am in Christ provided me with boldness and minimized my fear of rejection. For many years after becoming a Christian, I never knew how I should feel, connect or relate with Christ when partaking the communion sacrament of bread and wine. Rev. Dr. Brad Strait helped me understand through three sermon illustrations, pointing to Christ's sacrifice for me. The first was a true story referring to the *table of reconciliation*, symbolic of how we were reconciled to Christ, through His blood shed for us. A second symbolic reference was to what Rev. Strait called Christ's *table of grace*. And a third reference he made was to the *table of emptiness*—as Jesus emptied Himself. Having a deeper understanding for what Jesus did for me on the cross, I am more thankful, and communion has a greater impact. I am deeply indebted to Rev. Strait for helping me establish a firm foundation in Christ, understanding that we are intentional sinners under God's persistent grace. How rich and deep a blessing God's relationship was and is, was still lost on me. It was only after the security of my world was deeply shaken did I begin to understand. Sadly, after losing my first wife, Nancy, to breast cancer, there was a temptation to just "replace my loss" with a new relationship. But Rev. Dr. Don Sweeting encouraged me when he stated, "Our need for relational security is very real, and Jesus meets that need."

> "Our need for relational security is very real, and Jesus meets that need."
> —Rev. Dr. Don Sweeting

Because God initiated His relationship with me when He sent His Son Jesus, our relationship was made infinitely secure when I believed and received Him as my Savior. People come and go in our lives, but Jesus will never leave us. A fact that started to take hold in my life. We find hope and peace in the relational security of Jesus. One day I encountered Ian, an unbeliever, and we connected as we talked about Jesus. I asked how I could pray for him. He responded with one word, "Solitude." He concluded that the peace in Christ could meet his need for solitude. Christ can meet all our relationship needs, and I continue to hope than Ian will profess Him as his Savior. On another occasion, I offered a gospel handout to a sister in Christ named Savannah. I asked her if she would like another one, in case she knew anybody who was without hope. "I know a lot of people who are hopeless," she said, since she is a prison ministry leader at her Church. She was pleased to receive a quantity of gospel handouts to use in prison. Then there was the time a believing young lady named Amber was also happy to take a small quantity of gospel handouts, when I asked her if she knew anybody that was low on hope. What a blessing it has been for me to see God at work even through brief encounters with believers, to reach people I will probably never meet in places I will probably never go—using gospel handouts I was privileged to supply.

God greatly blessed me countless times through the relational ministry of Jesus, be it in a brief encounter, or prolonged relationships. There was a precious and profound moment at a rehabilitation hospital. On January 25, 2000 I was visiting Josh, a young quadriplegic, and his mother. His dream in flight school of being a fighter pilot was shattered after a tragic, alcohol related motorcycle accident at high speed. I asked him, "Describe your mother in one word." He struggled to write, "Mom." She said, "Can't you be more descriptive? Use an adjective." He then managed to write, "Here" twice, yet barely legible. He made his best effort to spell "Mom," and "Here." She asked, "You mean because I'm here?" He then gave her a "thumbs up."

We all need Jesus to be "here," to dwell with us. "...You are the God who sees me..." (Genesis 16:13); "...God is with us." (Isaiah 8:10); "And surely I am with you always,..." (Matthew 28:20) In the context of the disciples, author Robert E. Coleman wrote, "Amazing as it may seem, all Jesus did to teach these men His way was to draw them close to Himself... being 'with them'... they had 'continued with' Him..." (*The Master Plan of Evangelism*, pp. 41, 46) Also, author Mike Mason wrote, "Again and again Jesus exhorts us not only to listen to His words but to put them into practice, for by doing so we enter into a relationship with the author." (*Practicing the Presence of People*, p. 60)

I got to know a man named Jimmy through multiple brief encounters at a Christian homeless ministry. He was one of the kindest men I've ever known, a tiny, soft spoken man with long white hair. Sadly, he was beaten with a golf club by someone in the inner city who despised him. As far as I knew, his only possessions were a set of tools, which someone stole, leaving him with nothing beyond the clothes on his back. He loved to work on cars, but jobs were few and far between. Jimmy struggled with deep soul wounds from many years of abuse; even his mother called him a bastard. When Jimmy got anxious, he would hyperventilate, and I never knew what might happen next. Over time, God grew in us a blessed, joyful friendship. Sadly, one day, I saw my sin of insensitivity bubble up in a conversation we had. Jimmy had a great sense of humor which I greatly enjoyed. We challenged each other with questions about cars, and he knew far more than I. One day I jokingly said, "Jimmy, I'm really disappointed in you." Before I could finish the sentence with, "You haven't asked me a car question today," I saw his head sink in despair. At that very moment I realized, too late, how emotionally fragile his soul was. Apparently, all Jimmy heard was the word "disappointed." I unintentionally hurt his feelings. Hopefully I learned to be more discerning and empathetic, so as not to cause more emotional harm. When police warned Jimmy to move out of the city for his own protection because there were people who still wanted him dead, my wife and I quickly offered him a place to stay. He seldom left the bedroom while he was with us. Several days later, Jimmy was set to fly out of town to live with his daughter. Since he never flew before, I was so thankful God provided for him at the airport, miraculously calming his spirit. I stayed close by him, intently watching him, hopeful for his journey yet fearful that he would suffer a nervous breakdown before the flight. Whenever anything unexplained happened at the airline gate, he became severely intense, which affected his breathing. Over time, I tried to joyfully and proactively point Jimmy to Jesus, hoping he would exchange fear with faith in the only One who could save him.

When I was reading a true story from writer Karl Wheeler, it helped me understand how important even brief encounters can be in God's relational ministry work through us. He stated in part, "I'm hungry,' a voice cried from the shadow. Abruptly, a large woman emerged from the darkness and began her well-rehearsed pitch. I was able to catch only a few of the buzzwords in her staccato delivery: 'homeless,' 'broke,' and 'money.' 'What is your name?' I asked. 'Nadine.' 'She breathed Scotch." But in this case, Karl had not been a good gospel model, and he knew it. Two days later he got another chance, when he spotted her, yelling, "Hey, Nadine!' She asked, 'How do you know my name?' 'Nadine, I have exactly 18 cents in my pocket that you may have if you let me ask you one question. It will only take two minutes.' 'Let me have it,' she responded. 'If you were to die tonight, do you know where you would go, Nadine?' 'Hell. Straight to hell.' 'Why?' 'Because I am bad, very bad.' 'Hey, you who know my name so well,' she called after me as I left, 'will you give me a hug?' 'I returned and without speaking, held the poor woman tightly. Suddenly I knew why I was in D.C. enduring crowds. In a brief moment, I was part of the Gospel." (Abbreviated excerpts, September/October 1994 Youth for Christ newsletter)

My wife and I once attended a multicultural class at Church for several months, with segments taught by a friend named Nancy Buschart. One day, speaking within the context of suffering in the world, she stated, "The greatest suffering is separation from God." (Isaiah 59:2, Ephesians 4:18) This points to the crucial, relational ministry of Jesus. While I am secure in my relationship with Jesus, I can't help but think of those separated from God in their unbelief who suffer—often oblivious to the cause. Without Jesus, we are hopeless in quiet desperation, loneliness, and emptiness. Relationships we develop, albeit brief, God can use to end that suffering in those who are lost.

"The greatest suffering is separation from God."
—Nancy Buschart

A man who did snow removal at our house, Josh, had not been forthright in our business dealings. He told me that his wife left him, and that he had been depressed. I let him know I would be praying for him. He said, "I don't know how that works. I worship nature. I take off my shoes and put my feet on the ground. I worship the creation. I believe all religions are the same...except..." He just stopped mid-sentence, never finishing his thought. I don't know why. I hope Josh and I can reconnect someday. In the meantime, I pray for him, hoping he will come to a saving knowledge of Jesus Christ. Maybe our brief relationship was part of God's plan to plant that seed of salvation in Josh.

As God empowers me to love lost people, proclaiming the gospel, I hope it helps bring them joyfully to salvation one day. There is power in the gospel (Romans 1:16), the message woven throughout the Bible. [Credit: Pastor Alistair Begg] As I proclaim and preach divine truth, it is helpful for me to remember how Jesus used questions throughout His ministry. For example, Jesus asked, "Who is it you want?' 'What do you want me to do for you?' 'Do you want to get well?' 'Which is easier to say...?' 'Who do you say I am?" When Jesus asks questions, He is asking for relationship. [Adapted from Nancy Buschart]

It helps me better relate to people when I ask them questions. Jesus is also the great relational bridge builder. The allegorical character, Aslan [Christ] states in part, "...it lies across a river. But do not fear that, for I am the great

Bridge Builder. And now come; I will open the door in the sky and send you to your own land." (C.S. Lewis, *The Chronicles of Narnia*, p. 541) Nobody has to tell us to share wonderful news—we naturally want to tell others when we are in love with someone, when we love our grandchildren, etc.! Isn't being in a loving relationship with God wonderful news? God wants to fill our hearts with multiplied joy as we love others into the Kingdom of Heaven, by proclaiming the good news of Jesus—the best news ever! His light draws them, as we do His painstaking work. We need to point people to an encounter with Jesus.

> When Jesus asks questions, he is asking for relationship. —Adapted from Nancy Buschart.

One aspect of the relational ministry of Jesus was modeled in Jerusalem during the Festival of the Passover, when Joseph and Mary were looking for Him. "After three days they found Him in the temple courts, sitting among the teachers, listening to them and asking them questions. Everyone who heard Him was amazed at His understanding and His answers. When His parents saw Him, they were astonished. His mother said to Him, 'Son, why have you treated us like this? Your father and I have been anxiously searching for you.' 'Why were you searching for me?' He asked. 'Didn't you know I had to be in My Father's house?' But they did not understand what He was saying to them. Then He went down to Nazareth with them and was obedient to them. But His mother treasured all these things in her heart. And Jesus grew in wisdom and stature, and in favor with God and man." (Luke 2:46-52) Jesus, at an early age, understood who He was, His mission, and modeled the relative importance of His covenant-love relationship with His people—and the nuclear and extended family [adapted from Pastor Dave Strunk].

At times, I struggle with pride. One day at Church I was about to leave Bible study, when I was too proud to ask the men to pray for me regarding an endoscopy later that morning. But at that moment I desperately needed encouragement and prayer, so I said to an assistant, "I need a hug and a prayer," for which she was kind enough to provide both. She ended her prayer with, "...in the sweet and precious name of Jesus."—Proverbs 16:24 states, "Gracious words are a honeycomb, sweet to the soul and healing to the bones." About an hour and a half later I was fumbling with my clothes trying to get them all into a plastic bag as I was about to be prepped for the medical procedure. I grabbed two gospel handouts, not knowing to whom they would go. I gave them to nurse Jill, and as she placed them on the rolling table, I asked her to pass the other on to Kim. A third nurse, Karen, was about to insert the I.V. port in my arm, when she said, "She's more beautiful than me," referring to Jill. I said, "Why would you say something like that? You are beautiful in the eyes of God." Moments later God joyfully blessed me as I watched Karen pick up the gospel handout that Jill placed on the table. She began to read it, and in that moment, God did something I could not. As I drove away from the doctor's office in tears that day, I regretted my spiritual pride, not fully trusting God—yet thankful for what He did in that office. It's humbling to know that, apart from Jesus, I can do nothing.

There are many times God has interceded to naturally and wonderfully transition a secular conversation to an opportunity for spiritual connection with someone. Once I was on the telephone with a bright young lady named Malana, confirming hotel reservations. After a brief attempt to pronounce her name, she said, "Think banana." As the conversation continued, I learned she had experience in both the nonprofit and for-profit business sectors. Malana mentioned a nonprofit organization that trained handicapped people, using horse therapy. I spoke of my familiarity with an organization named Praying Hands Ranch, where my wife received horse therapy after her brain stem stroke. That simple, common connection allowed me the opportunity to steer our conversation to Jesus. Malana was still searching for her path in life, and as a result she would be leaving her current position in two days for another hotel job. I asked if I could pray for her after I hung up, that God would guide her in her direction and decisions. She said yes. As our conversation ended, I said, "Malana, Jesus loves you very much." "That sounds good," she said. I hoped to meet her on the last day of her job, but that didn't work out. Perhaps God will allow someone to water the seed I was allowed to plant. God is trustworthy, and He can make it grow. He will provide a way when there isn't one. Thank you, Lord, for these unexpected blessings. I do not think it is a coincidence that the first two devotional scriptures I read right after this conversation were, "In his heart a man plans his course, but the LORD determines his steps," (Proverbs 16:9) and "Blessed is the man who does not walk in the counsel of the wicked or stand in the way of sinners or sit in the seat of mockers. But his delight is in the law of the Lord, and on His law, he meditates day and night." (Psalm 1:1-2)

Relationships are incredibly important, and there is power in Christ's relational ministry. Chaplain Tim Boettger stated, "The Creator designed us to live in community. Jesus commissioned us to 'love one another even as I have loved you.' (John 13:34) Tim went on to say, 'Need more proof? A recent Harvard study followed more than 700 participants for 75 years. It determined the root of happiness is not money, fame or good looks—it's our relationships.' The study director summed it up by saying, 'The clearest message...is this: Good relationships keep us happier and healthier. Period." (Western Home Communities—*The Journal*, May 2019, p. 6)

It was a cold, clear day on the trail and I was not expecting to see many people, so I grabbed just one gospel handout. I passed a lady in a purple coat who had a friendly reply when I said hello. I hoped to see her again, so I could offer her the gospel handout. As I neared the end of a beautiful walk, I crossed paths with her at the intersection of two trails. I said, "I bin sav'n this for you!" She looked surprised, but I quickly repeated how another lady explained that, "Love and the cross are one and the same," as I showed her the handout. She introduced herself as Peggy, and she was thankful to receive it. In that moment, God brought a joyful blessing to both of us. Maybe one day I will know how God worked through that brief encounter. On another cold day, my wife waited in the car while I hurried in to pick up her prescription. Everything went well, so I headed to the men's restroom where I placed three gospel handouts, having faith that God would put them to good use. I left the restroom with one in hand thinking, "I'll just keep it in my hand and if it is not given to someone, I'll take it to the car." As I was heading toward the door, I walked by the customer service counter. I noticed the lady customer service representative tried to get my attention. Surprised, I had no idea what she wanted. She asked me if I dropped a receipt. I didn't think so, because the pharmacist always staples it to the bag. She asked if I had just been to the pharmacy. I said, "Yes." She asked if the last four digits of the credit card matched mine, which they did. That never happened to me before. She told me that a young girl saw it on the floor, picked it up, and took it to the customer service counter. Rose, the customer service lady, handed me my receipt. I thanked her for returning it, and in exchange I handed her a gospel handout. She stared at it momentarily, looked up at me and broke down in tears. She said, "I needed that." I asked if I could pray for her. She said, "Yes." I asked how. She said, "He knows." As I left, she was reading the gospel handout, which I sometimes see people do. I started praying for her as I joyfully left the store, knowing this brief encounter was a divine appointment orchestrated by God.

chapter 5
Joyful Imperative

When I went to bed, I knew I was stuck, struggling to get a handle on what to write, trying to build Biblical evidence—the rationale for spreading the gospel message. I was spiritually paralyzed from my inability to move forward without an inspiration from God. Nothing I wrote seemed to help. As I laid in bed early the next morning, I began to meditate in my spirit and mind on what I called the *foundational mandate*—to glorify God; and then I contrasted it with what I called the *mission mandate*—to proclaim God. I got out of bed, went into my study, bowed down to God and prayed. There seemed to emerge words from God which I needed, to press on toward the goal—I wrote as the Holy Spirit led. I double checked a Bible study handout from two days before, when Bible teacher and hospice Chaplain Bryan Mackey stated in part, "Justification is the primary, fundamental blessing of the gospel; it meets our most basic spiritual need—forgiveness and reconciliation with God." (Galatians chapters 3 and 4) God also seemed to clarify what I call His joyful imperative—the integration and mysterious correlation between proclaiming God's message of our salvation (Ephesians 1:13), occasional suffering as a result, and His emerging blessed deep, sacred "Jesus Joy." I went back to bed around 5:00 a.m., content in Christ alone, despite the world's chaos and confusion.

But why the imperative, along with joy? Why does God's Word express a command in association with spreading the gospel? Because God gave me the desire to proclaim the gospel and filled me with such joy is so doing, I wanted to theologically capture and document the Biblical rationale for giving a mandate in reference to spreading the good news. I felt if I could clearly see and be sure of the correlation between how God convicted me, what I experienced, and that it is in line with the truth of His Holy Word, I could more effectively be Christ's witness. I reexamined the scriptural mandate for preaching the gospel, and then sought out many viewpoints on the subject, including Biblical commentators, Pastors, Evangelists, and Theologians.

It was helpful to me when Author Robert E. Coleman stated, in part, "The Great Commission of Christ given to His church summed it up in the command to "make disciples of every creature," (Matthew 28:19) in his book *The Master Plan of Evangelism,* second edition, abridged, p. 101. The word here indicates that the disciples were to go out into the world and win others who would come to be what they themselves were—disciples of Christ. This mission is emphasized even more when the Greek text of the passage is studied, and it is seen that the words *go, baptize,* and *teach* are all participles which derive their force from the one controlling verb "make disciples. This means that the great commission is not merely to go to the ends of the Earth preaching the gospel (Mark 16:15),..." Coleman reinforced the imperative by going on to state, in part, in the Endnotes, of the reference cited, "I am indebted to Dr. Roland G. Leavell for first calling this to my attention in his book *Evangelism, Christ's Imperative Commission* (Nashville: Broadman Press, 1951), p. 3. The participle "go," however, does stand in a coordinate relationship with the verb which makes it also an imperative."

But what is it about God's infinitely majestic character that inspires me to know, love, praise, worship, serve and proclaim Him? As I gathered commentaries, I gradually built a *quiet confidence* [Credit: Rev. David Baer], that God's painstaking joyful journey for me to proclaim the gospel, was spelled out in scores, and even hundreds, of clear Biblical passages. I asked one of my favorite Bible teachers, Pastor Dave Strunk, to help capture the essential character of God, and shed some light on the rationale in response to my question, "Why should I sacrificially take a risk to proclaim Christ's gospel of peace?" It was a great encouragement to me when he encapsulated the following, "Jesus is the subject of the Bible from beginning to end. He created all things and in Him all things hold together. He's the heir of Eve to destroy the head of the Serpent. He's the true offspring of Abraham that will bless all nations. He fulfills the perfection of God's covenant with Moses. He is the true and greatest prophet, priest, and king. And He is very God of very God come to earth as fully human to die for us and rise to new life for us. He is the supreme God of the universe who lived for us. It should astonish us that we could even know Him, and that He'd let us know Him. Even more, we can share Him with others. He is the fact of history that the world must know about."

Pastor Dave's Biblical teaching helped me to be thankful when I responded to the Holy Spirit's leading to approach a young man at the light rail station on my way to work. This man, Mike, was so covered with tattoos, I could see not one square inch of his skin that was not tattooed. I was initially shocked and fearful at the sight of his body tattoos—I stood about ten feet away from him for a few moments. I didn't know how to respond. Mysteriously, God gave me enough courage to walk up and speak with him, while inside I dreaded the possible response. I gave Mike a scripture-based gospel handout as I spoke with him. Then God began to connect us relationally, and He showed me the heart of one of the gentlest men I've ever met—a believer and follower of Jesus. Mike came out of the drug culture, and now used those deficits as blessings to proactively spread the gospel to people with whom he related. God filled both of our hearts with great joy that day! I am eternally grateful the Holy Spirit empowered me to engage with Mike. We parted ways, but I wish I could reconnect with him again.

To spread the gospel, I searched for encouragement from God and was thankful for numerous insightful words written by Tim Beougher, the Billy Graham Professor of Evangelism and Associate Dean of the Billy Graham School at the Southern Baptist Theological Seminary in Louisville, Kentucky. These numerous, brief excerpts were helpful to me, as Tim stated in part, "Church members sometimes wonder if they should just leave evangelism to the 'professionals.' After all, isn't evangelism a spiritual gift?' 'Some argue that the Great Commission was only given to the apostles and therefore does not apply to us today. While it is true that contextually the Great Commission (Matthew 28:18-20) was given *to* the apostles, it was not *only* for the apostles.' 'What had

Jesus commanded the apostles? Among many other things, He commanded them to preach the gospel to the whole creation. So, this command of Jesus given to the apostles also applies to every believer today.' 'Some claim that since only some people have the "gift of evangelism," not everyone is obligated to witness' 'First, evangelism is not recorded in the common spiritual gifts listings in Scripture; instead, the office of evangelist is mentioned in Ephesians 4:11. Some (myself included) question whether "evangelism" should be seen as a distinct spiritual gift, such as giving, serving, and so on. In addition, even if evangelism is a spiritual gift, it is also a command for all believers, just like giving, serving, and so on. Not having "the gift of evangelism" does not excuse a believer from his or her call to share Christ with others." "The commands to witness are given to all followers of Christ. Acts 1:8, for example, reads, "But you will receive power when the Holy Spirit has come upon you, and you will be My witnesses in Jerusalem and in all Judea and Samaria, and to the ends of the earth." This verse gives a command from the risen Lord to all His followers. As John Stott argues, "We can no more restrict the command to witness than we can restrict the promise of the Spirit."

I appreciate what Tim says in the following excerpts, because I am just an ordinary laborer sent forth into the harvest, "Consider the example of "ordinary believers" in the early church. As we follow the storyline of the early church it is obvious that the apostles sought to evangelize and disciple others. But we see ordinary believers proclaiming the gospel as well. Following the stoning of Stephen, we read Acts 8:1, "And there arose on that day a great persecution against the church in Jerusalem, and they were all scattered throughout the regions of Judea and Samaria, except the apostles." And what did those ordinary believers do? Acts 8:4 tells us: "Now those who were scattered went about preaching (*euangelizomenoi*) the word." They went about proclaiming the gospel with others. Noted historian Kenneth Scott Latourette makes this observation about the spread of the gospel: The chief agents in the expansion of Christianity appear not to have been those who made it a profession or a major part of their occupation, but men and women who earned their livelihood in some purely secular manner and spoke of their faith to those whom they met in this natural fashion." "Consider the stewardship the gospel imposes on us. Jesus reminds us, "Everyone to whom much was given, of him much will be required." (Luke 12:48) We have been given no greater gift than the gospel, and we have no greater stewardship than to share that message of good news with others. Paul expresses it well in 2 Corinthians 5:14: "for the love of Christ controls us."

Tim also encouraged Pastors, with the following exhortation, "Pastors, we can say to our people with confidence, "you are called to be a witness for Christ in both word and deed." As leaders, let us challenge other believers not only with our exhortations but also with our example. And let us take great confidence in the gospel, "for it is the power of God for salvation to everyone who believes, to the Jew first and also to the Greek." (Romans 1:16)

Tim's writing was very helpful to me in clarifying the often-quoted scripture from 1 Peter 3:15, in the context of, "...be prepared to give an answer..." "While the context of 1 Peter 3:15 is what can be called "passive evangelism" (responding to a question that an unbeliever asks), this command is clearly given to all believers "to be ready" to answer when asked. [Also, 1 Peter 3 in context of the "passive" words regarding, "...be prepared to give an answer..." points to the surrounding text involving people doing harm or evil to believers who are doing what is right.] (*Must Every Christian Evangelize?* 9Marks Journal, Part 1, August 27, 2013)

I am deeply indebted and thankful to Evangelist Bill Fay, who shared the gospel with over 25,000 people over many years. He stated "I have found that the average Christian heard the gospel 7.6 times before surrendering to Christ..." (*Share Jesus Without Fear*, p. 10) Since I don't know people's spiritual condition, where they are on their journey, I am compelled by God to proclaim the good news of Jesus, as the Holy Spirit leads me.

Regarding Hebrews 12:2, in the context of joy, a brief excerpt from *Ellicott's Commentary for English Readers* stated, "Who for the joy that was set before Him endured the cross.—The literal meaning is very forcible, *endured a cross, despising shame*; the shame of such a death being set over against the joy that lay before Him." *Benson Commentary* reinforced this with, "...Where there is fullness of joy for evermore." And the *Pulpit Commentary* sheds more light on this joy stating, "To the true Christian the grand inspiring principle is still the love of God and of his neighbor, and of goodness for its own sake, though the hope of an eternal reward supports and cheers him mightily. Nor, again, is the joy looked forward to a selfish joy. It is the joy of sharing in the triumph of eternal righteousness in company with all the redeemed, whose salvation, no less than his own, he desires and strives for. And, further, with regard to his own individual joy, what is it but the joy of attaining the end of his being, the perfection God meant him for, and to which it is his duty to aspire? Hence Christ would not have been a perfect example to man had He not been represented as looking forward to 'the joy that was set before Him.'"

It was helpful to me when I considered two key Biblical scriptures regarding Christ's command to preach the gospel. First, Matthew 28:19, "Therefore go and make disciples of all nations, baptizing them in the name of the Father and of the Son and of the Holy Spirit," A brief excerpt from the Benson commentary on Matthew 28:19, 20 stated, "Our Lord's words, taken together, in both verses, distinctly enjoin three things, and that in the following order, [Greek words excluded] that is, to proselyte men to Christ, to baptize, and to teach them." And a brief excerpt from the Matthew Henry commentary on Matthew 28:16-20 stated, "He now solemnly commissioned the apostles and His ministers to go forth among all nations. The salvation they were to preach, is a common salvation; whoever will, let him come, and take the benefit; all are welcome to Christ Jesus." Secondly, Mark 16:15 stated, "He said to them, "Go into all the world and preach the gospel to all creation." A brief excerpt from the Benson Commentary on Mark 16:15, 16 stated, "*Go ye into all the world*—To all countries under heaven; *and preach the gospel to every creature*—That is, to all mankind, to every human being, whether Jew or Gentile, for our Lord speaks without any limitation or restriction whatever. On this Bengelius remarks, "If all men, of all places and ages, have not heard the gospel, the successors of the first preachers, or those whose duty it was to hear it, have not answered God's design herein, but have made void His counsel."

The following statement was insightful for me, "The missionary enterprise has been put on many bases. People do not like commandments, but yet it is a great relief and strength to come back to one and answer all questions with

'He bids me!" (*MacLaren's Expositions* commentary (THE WORLD-WIDE COMMISSION) for Mark 16:15. An excerpt from *Vincent's Word Studies* stated in part, "The joy was the full, divine beatitude of His preincarnate life in the bosom of the Father; the glory which He had with God before the world was. In exchange for this He accepted the cross and the blame. The contrast is designed between the struggle which, for the present, is alone set before the readers (Hebrews 12:1), and the joy which was already present to Christ. The heroic character of His faith appears in His renouncing a joy already in possession in exchange for shame and death. The passage thus falls in with Philippians 2:6-8."

If I was spiritually lost, destined for hell, where the fire never goes out (Matthew 25:41, Mark 9:43, et. al.), and a believer looked into the eyes of my heart seeing my desperate condition, I would have begged them to proclaim the joyful gospel of peace to me, knowing that I am subject to the *double resurrection* [Credit: Pastor Mark Brewer], some to eternal life and others to eternal condemnation. (Daniel 2:12, John 5:29, Matthew 25:46, et. al.)

chapter 6
Reluctant Obedience

God often grants me great joy when people thankfully receive a gospel handout, because of the potential impact God can make. But some people resist, like the young man at the counter who said, "I always turn these down," as I offered him the gospel handout. "Save it for somebody else," the lady said. Another said "I'm good." And another, "I'm OK." When I asked a bright young man in the process of changing jobs how I could pray for him, he sadly told me, "I'm not a praying man." And a lady said, "I don't like the dying system," whatever that was supposed to mean. After she received a gospel handout, I asked a psychology major named Kaitlyn, "Do you think psychology needs theology to reach its full potential?" "No! Psychology is science. They haven't found commonality between the two so they can coexist," she defiantly said. Dick, a family relative, told my brother Bruce, "I don't trust the Church." Bruce, who is also a Pastor, said, "Get in Aunt Mildred's Church." "It's not working for me," Dick replied. Bruce told him, "You need to feed your soul or you'll die; just like your stomach." A neighbor, Bryan, once told me he believes, "Life ends when you die; your spirit goes up, with . . . I've got good karma. You can't know until you're dead." Sadly, Bryan died in his sleep, but not before our neighbor proclaimed the good news of Jesus to him just hours before. So he heard the good news. We don't know if he accepted it, but God does. While we looked up at the beautiful clouds, a friend of mine said, "For those of you who are of a religious persuasion . . ." I pray and hope he will be eternally with me in

God's presence. A long-time school friend struggling with cancer said, "I wish you good health. That is the best we can have." Jesus offers her even better! Once while walking along a riverbank in Alaska, I met a man and tried to offer him spiritual blessings. He replied, "Family trumps everything." Stunned, I could not think of anything to say. I saw him again a few more times. I also saw his wife during Sunday morning worship, but he was nowhere to be seen.

Perhaps due to fear of rejection, there were times I was reluctant in proclaiming the gospel and have confessed, "God, I really don't want to do this." However, God showed me that rejection is never as bad as the loss of joy from not sharing, along with the sadness from regret that inevitably follows. I may reluctantly start, but I am thankful afterwards, as I am greatly blessed along with the person I gave the gospel. A young man with whom I crossed paths on the trail as I walked, responded to my greeting warmly, with a smile. I hoped to see him again. Upon heading for home on the trail, I saw him again, and he again kindly responded. He said something like, "Hello, again!" But I didn't turn around, catch his attention, engage him with conversation, and hopefully give him the gift of God's Word. I missed the opportunity to share—followed by regret. And I hadn't prayed while on the trail in advance to prepare for what God might bring. God doesn't need me, but I need Him, because most responses are unique. I never know what someone will do or say. I never know what God is going to do, but in His lovingkindness, He allows me to be a part of His divine plan and share the good news with others.

My reluctance to proclaim the gospel—my disobedience to God's call—reminds me of a story by author Brian A. Williams, about a fourth century Pastor, Gregory of Nazianzus. "Who is prepared to respond to the call to pastoral ministry in Christ's Church? No one, if he will listen to my judgment and accept my advice! This is of all things most to be feared, this is the most extreme of dangers in the eyes of everyone who understands the magnitude of success and the utter ruin of failure!" (*The Potter's Rib*, p. 13, 14) In like manner, who is prepared to respond to the call to proclaim the gospel? No one, without God's grace and mentoring!

I was a short distance from home late one afternoon, just starting to walk on my usual trail. While standing by a fence overlooking the small stream down below, I gazed into the sky where there was a beautiful storm cloud moving from the mountains. I tried to fully absorb the magnitude of all that it represented. This helped open up a pleasant conversation with a woman named Ruth, who approached on the trail. We talked about meteorological cloud development, among other topics. After offering Ruth the gospel handout for a second time, she kindly received God's Word, and we joyfully parted ways. A little further downhill along the trail, I approached three young boys sitting on a wooden bench. Coming up from behind them, I felt like there was no chance to spiritually relate to them, partly out of intimidation and fear of the unknown. So I slowly passed them, but reluctantly stopped about 10 to 15 feet beyond, and greeted them. I remained at a distance, so as not to alarm them, but also being totally dependent upon God for the courage to engage them. As we began to talk, I learned that their names were Rylan, Serea, and Josh—all three young high school age boys. They were a lot like me when I was their age, lacking direction and purpose. All three seemed open to continuing the conversation, which pleasantly surprised me. So, I drew a little closer to them, and we found numerous connections on which we could relate. I asked them, "Will you do me a big favor?" They nodded. I asked if I could show them the red heart and cross graphic and tell them the story of how it came about. They happily agreed. Later, all three graciously accepted a gospel handout, and I soon found myself joyfully thanking them for uplifting me. I

I don't want to face Christ's judgement in heaven, if I haven't proclaimed Him on Earth.

was so blessed when they said the same to me! God lovingly delivered me from my reluctance. I don't want to face Christ's judgement in heaven, if I haven't proclaimed Him on Earth.

One day I decided to walk to deliver a letter to a neighbor, pay a bill and send a letter from the post office. To prepare for the walk, I placed gospel handouts in my billfold, and three flat, unfolded gospel handouts in my hand, to place strategically in the post office. I'm sure I've been on lots of their surveillance cameras! But God had other plans. When I hit the trail, two young girls already walking converged with me on the trail. I greeted them, and we spoke briefly. I asked if I might bless them with good news. They were very kind, friendly and both joyfully said, "Sure." I wasn't expecting that encounter, but I was so thankful God prepared me for it, joyfully blessing them and me! Smiling, the two girls left, and I continued on to the post office. As I waited in line at the post office, I spoke with the lady behind me, Amy. She was very kind, with a nice smile. I asked her if I could bless her with good news, as I offered her a gospel handout. She looked at it as she got out her glasses and asked, "What is it?" I said, "Many years ago God gave me this red heart and cross graphic—one lady who looked at it said, 'Love and the cross are one and the same.'" She was quick to agree. I told her that the rest of the gospel handout contained Bible verses. I asked her if she was a follower of Jesus and she radiantly said she was. I then asked, "Is there anyone you might want to offer this to, that is in need of hope?" She shocked me when she said, "Yes, the whole [name deleted] High School." Because of her tone of voice, it was immediately apparent that she was going to share something grave. Two student suicides had just occurred within 72 hours at the same school, where two lives were taken just a few years prior—an extra heavy blow. She asked if I would pray for them, to which of course I agreed. If the Holy Spirit had not prompted me to proclaim God's Word with her, I wouldn't have known to start praying for the high school, as well as for our neighborhood friends and their two children, both of whom attend that school. The next day I had to get a recalled airbag on the car repaired and the dealer told me they would need the car all day. So, I asked the courtesy car driver to drop me off by the school where the suicides occurred. I was convicted to go. I didn't want to go. I lacked courage, but I had to obey God, even in reluctance. While we were on our way to the school, the driver shared with me his pain of suffering through a divorce. I asked him if he would allow me to tell him what Jesus did in my life. He agreed, thanked me afterward, and agreed that what Jesus did for me made sense.

As I was dropped off across the street from the school, I felt awkward. I was especially uncomfortable in the presence of a police car, sheriff's car, two sheriff deputies walking by me, hundreds of cars passing, and sensing that the people drinking coffee on the restaurant patio seemed to be watching me. Additionally, there were hundreds of students taking their lunch break from school, walking by me towards the shopping center. I stepped out in faith, but to help settle my spirit, I started by offering gospel handouts outside a grocery store. There, I spoke to a student, "I'm sorry about your loss of two students." I don't remember much of a response, but at least it was a reluctant start toward obedience to God. I stalled long enough and retraced my steps back to the school. I stood by the crosswalk light, directly across the street from the school. As I spoke with students and offered them gospel handouts, I noticed they were rather quiet, somber and subdued, but very kind and friendly, with warm, radiant smiles. To my surprise, they were extremely thankful as we exchanged fragile words. God began to bless me, especially seeing that the students were so thankful. It was as if they saw that an adult really cared about them—that they were not just alone. After I ran out of gospel handouts, I walked and prayed around much of the school. As I walked along the school fence, I came across a purple sticky note on the ground. It had two words written on it, along with a drawing of a small heart, "Stay Strong!"

It was as if they saw that an adult really cared about them— that they were not just alone.

Ironically, two young Mormons on bicycles were waiting at the intersection light with me as I headed home. They asked about my day. I responded that I was praying and proclaiming the gospel with students after their loss. The Mormons had something nice to say, then headed off on their bikes seemingly detached from the gravity of the situation. In a conversation with one of my wife's caregivers, the question was raised about why I was not prohibited from being on school property when I prayed and walked. Her experience had been that their school was always under "lock down." But God provides ways to spread the gospel—because even if schools were under special security protocols, without God, the schools and students have no hope. I need to do the hard, gut work of the gospel, even if people oppose me. Exodus 19:8 states, in part, " . . .We will do everything the Lord has said." My wife later shared 1 Corinthians 15:58 with me, "Therefore, my dear brothers and sisters, stand firm. Let nothing move you. Always give yourselves fully to the work of the Lord, because you know that your labor in the Lord is not in vain."

During our Church's domestic missions Sunday, I spoke with my friend Chuck Lewis, a hospital Chaplain, about my frequent lack of obedience— disobeying God, especially in the presence of opposition. On the spot, he coined the term "reluctant obedience." He said he often prayed before seeing a patient, "Lord, if you don't show up, I'm in trouble." Chuck had a lot of challenges in his life, but he is a great overcomer in Christ. I hope to speak with him further to learn more about the "why" of reluctant obedience.

"Lord, if you don't show up, I'm in trouble." —hospital Chaplain Chuck Lewis

While hiking late one afternoon, several people gathered on the trail to watch a beautiful bald eagle high in the tree. In 15 years of hiking this trail, this was my first bald eagle encounter. I brought one gospel handout with me, not expecting to see many people. As several of us watched the eagle, a lady named Michelle was kind enough to receive the gospel handout. As dusk set in, I started home, but there was a young man still watching the eagle, so we briefly chatted. I soon realized that I did not have another gospel handout with me, but I sensed an opportunity to testify about my faith in Jesus. I was reluctant. I don't know why. As conviction grew, I knew I needed to proclaim my faith in Jesus to him, gospel handout or no gospel handout. But he started down the trail again. I quickly realized I lost my opportunity and failed to trust God. This was inexcusable because God opened the perfect door of ministry when this man expressed disappointment in his college team losing the big football game that would have placed them in the national championship. What a wonderful transition that would have made for me to proclaim the comfort, provision and love of Jesus. As I headed home, I thought, "Am I going to have to spend the rest of my life continuing to learn these difficult lessons?" I was very disappointed in myself for failing to proclaim the gospel. Ironically, it was so intuitively obvious to everyone gathered on the trail, to share the good news of the eagle with everyone passing. And we did! There wasn't one person on the trail who didn't hear that good news. Because of my hesitation I exchanged joy for sadness.

On a grocery run, I called my wife from the car, while parked in the store parking lot. I sometimes pray and read God's Word at length in the car, since there are few distractions, but this time I was reluctant. I told her I was afraid to pray because God often does something amazing that may require my obedience. I was resisting the Holy Spirit. Acts 7:51 states, "You stiff-necked people! Your hearts and ears are still uncircumcised! You are just like your ancestors: You always resist the Holy Spirit!"

On another occasion when I approached this same store, I walked over to drop something into the large trash barrel outside on the patio. A young man wearing a baseball cap and sunglasses sat there reading with his head slumped in a chair. "Good morning," I said. I thought I heard a faint grunt in response, as he seemed unwilling to communicate. I had a gospel handout ready to give him but walked past him toward the front door of the store. Within 15 feet, the Holy Spirit convicted me to turn around and hand him God's Word. I thought I would just take the chance and offer him the gospel handout, but I never thought he would actually take it. I reluctantly asked, "May I give you a gift of good news?"

> "You stiff-necked people! Your hearts and ears are still uncircumcised! You are just like your ancestors: You always resist the Holy Spirit!"
> —Acts 7:51

I was joyfully surprised when he said, "Please," imperatively—seemingly almost begging. His name was Davin. As we talked, he seemed very thoughtful and intellectually curious, asking me many spiritual questions. It was funny how he asked a question and then drew his own conclusions before I could respond. Davin seemed to express that he didn't need to be accountable for his behavior, actions or lifestyle, because of God's good nature, allowing for any and all shortcomings. He worked at a sandwich shop, confessed that he sold "weed," and felt he was "stuck," destined for a life of *boredom* and *doubt*. God began to create a connection between us as we talked. Davin became very open and willing to discuss deeper spiritual matters. We talked together for at least an hour and a half. Contrary to the devil trying to convince me that I could not defend my faith, God gave me scriptural responses to his many questions. God was doing most all the work and I was sort of just along for the ride! We spoke a lot about how to "know" that you can have eternal life, as opposed to eternal condemnation. I asked him to read out loud from 1 John 5:10-13. I expected him to stop reading at that point—mysteriously, he kept on reading, so I kept listening and praying silently. Three verses later after reading, "There is a sin that leads to death," he stopped dead in his tracks, silent, then said, "Oh, no." He was visibly and audibly stunned, paralyzed. Despite all his intellectual thinking, he realized that his sin of unbelief led to spiritual death. [I believe at that precise moment; it was Holy Spirit conviction.] As I got ready to head into the store, I asked him if he would like to join my wife and me in worship that coming Sunday. He said, "Please!" [again, imperatively—seemingly almost begging] Assuring me he would attend Church on Sunday, it did not come to fruition, nor have I been able to meet with him. I am still hopeful and continue inviting him to reconnect with me. I felt compelled by the Holy Spirit, so I left Davin a telephone message in reference to Hebrews 9:27, offering him the truth about being accountable to God for our life. Our conversation seemed similar to one I had with a neighbor, as I tried to proclaim the gospel. He said he believed in Western mysticism—that when you die, it's over. I don't know if his lack of faith in Jesus was true doubt or false doubt—wishful thinking. In another instance, when I offered a man a gospel handout, he responded, "I'm OK." He said when he died, he would go "in the ground." I responded, "No, I mean your spirit." "I don't know," he said.

One day after praying in the car by a grocery store, I called my wife. After saying goodbye, I looked up and saw a man smoking a cigarette in the cold. I said, "Lord, I really don't want to do this." I got out of the car, walked slowly over to him, and asked if I could offer him some good news. "Anytime!" He said his name was Tony, and he was wonderfully kind. As he walked away, he had his head down reading it. God's amazing love for people continued in the store, with Mike, an employee, receiving the gospel handout. He looked at me in disbelief because he just moved here, and a friend encouraged him to get involved spiritually. He asked for the name of our Church and where it was located. I was thankful that God yet again showed me His amazing love for others, this time with a young single working Mother, Casey and her daughter Tanner. Casey was so grateful to receive God's Word. I was thankful and humbled that God would allow me to be used in this manner. I still pray for Casey.

Too often God has to humble me in a pejorative sense when proclaiming the gospel, especially when I don't pray and listen to Him. I spoke with a woman on the trail named Dottie, who seemed very kind and friendly. I tried to pull out one gospel handout but botched it. Instead of just one handout, out of my pocket came the plastic holder along with several gospel handouts! I was so embarrassed, but she was still kind enough to receive God's Holy Word. Another time, God showed me an example of my need for total dependence upon Him. While waiting at the checkout counter, I placed a gospel handout upside down near my purchased items as a reminder. Lisa cheerfully helped me check out, but she was weak from cancer surgery and treatment. Her employer allowed her to sit on a stool to conserve her energy. She used a basket on the first section of the counter to prevent people from putting purchases out of her reach. When I moved my items to the other side of this basket, I forgot about the gospel handout I placed there. After we had a blessed conversation and I handed her another gospel handout, she noticed the previous one I left. She said, "Is that for the next person?" I was saddened that she asked that question. I assured her that it was specifically for her. I hoped she did not feel like an "impersonal number." I wished I was more prayerful, with better situational awareness and preparation. Even though God brought joy to both of us, I believe I limited the impact of my witness by not drawing closer to God.

God showed me that hospitals are often fertile ground for bearing good fruit that will last (John 15), and opening up doors of ministry (Acts 14:27, 1 Corinthians 16:9 and 2 Corinthians 2:12). Many years ago, I walked out of an inner-city hospital, after spending time comforting patients. Once outside, I passed a young lady sitting on a step, seemingly downcast. Not ten feet past her, the Holy Spirit led me to go back and speak with her. Her name was Maria. I offered a gospel handout, and asked her to read the verses out loud, as evangelist Bill Fey recommends. I was thrilled with what God did. She joyfully confessed believing and receiving Jesus Christ as her Savior. "I've been waiting a long time for this," Maria shared. She mentioned that her uncle was a Pastor. We continued speaking briefly as she shared a little about her life, and then we joyfully parted ways. Unfortunately, Maria opened the door for further spiritual communication, but I failed to follow up. I regret not continuing our dialogue over time—certainly I could have stayed in touch by phone, to encourage her in her young faith—please forgive me, Lord. I live with the sadness of my spiritual failure. But in that brief moment I witnessed a powerful example of God's kingdom of heaven work on Earth. I reluctantly obeyed. It was all God's work. I'm so thankful that God chose to use me as His lowly servant so I could see His work. I read about a Vietnamese Christian Pastor imprisoned for his faith, who stated, "We have learned that suffering is not the worst thing in the world—disobedience to God is the worst." (*Extreme Devotion*, p. 7, The Voice of the Martyrs)

In hospital parking garages, the smell of cigarette smoke can become overpowering. I sometimes look around to see where it is coming from, and see the person smoking in their car or standing alongside it. In one instance, I got out of my car to go inside the hospital to visit my wife, when I smelled the strong, acrid scent of cigarette smoke. As I walked by the woman smoking, I greeted her and she smiled kindly in response. I rushed past, when the Holy Spirit started to convict me. The inevitable internal struggle ensued. "I don't have time for this," I thought, "my wife is waiting." As so often happens, in the end it comes down to the difference between *eternal consequences* and *temporary inconvenience.*

> "In the end it comes down to the difference between eternal consequences and temporary inconvenience."
> —Frank Ballesteri

My wife, and the time I get to spend with her is God's gift, a gift I should never abuse, take for granted, or raise above the Giver. Now fully convicted, the Holy Spirit turned me around, in spite of my reluctance to proclaim the gospel. Because the Holy Spirit provided me the strength and courage, I went back and thanked the woman for blessing me with her smile and kindness. I introduced myself. She said her name was Michelle. I asked her if I could bless her with good news, as I handed her a gospel handout. She was very gracious, warmly received it, and thanked me for it. We parted ways with both of us doubly blessed by a brief, and friendly encounter. On these occasions I am often filled with joy and thanked God that His Word does not return void or empty (Isaiah 55:11). God seems to use me mostly to sow or plant the seed of the gospel, as I trust Him for others to "water" it, but for Him to make it grow (1 Corinthians 3:6, 7).

In 2008, as my wife and I struggled to make a three-month commitment to serve overseas in a country hostile to Jesus Christ, we worshipped in a small mountain Church one Sunday. The guest speaker was Dr. Lew Sterrett, a horse trainer and evangelist—*Sermon on the Mount* ministry. We talked with him after his message and mentioned our need to make a decision about a three-month commitment overseas. He quietly listened, and then said, "When the pain of not taking action exceeds the risk, you might as well go for it!" After hearing his words of wisdom, our decision came easy. While we prepared for the trip, Pastor Marty Martin called one day and asked how we were doing. I was so thankful at that moment, because his call brought much needed comfort. I said, "I'm nervous and Barbie's edgy!" We reluctantly obeyed God's call to serve in a difficult land, which was very hard, yet very good for us at the same time. God blessed us beyond measure once we stepped out in faith for Jesus.

> "Never lose hope that God can, and live and rest in the tension that he may or may not."
> —Pastor Dave Strunk

The Apostle Paul stated, "I came to you in weakness with great fear and trembling." (1 Corinthians 2:3) And Jesus said, "Apart from me you can do nothing." Clearly, I am dependent upon God to do His work. Pastor Dave Strunk stated, "Never lose hope that God can, and live and rest in the tension that he may or may not."

In context of the aforementioned word "tension," Jared Kelso interjected the adjective "healthy," as in "healthy tension." I thanked him for shedding spiritual light on the difficult topic of spiritual tension. The truth about ourselves is that we can't proclaim the gospel in our own strength. We need God's help. At a men's prayer encounter, a man confessed that he could not proclaim the gospel, and stated, "I can't do it." Dr. Kent Hutcheson, the speaker, responded, "You're right—I can't either, without God's help, through the power of the Holy Spirit." Genesis 41:16 states in part, "I cannot do it, . . . but God will . . ." Forgive me Lord for becoming battle weary.

I'm always grateful to God when people receive His Word. In the bank one day, I spoke with a young lady named Destiny, the bank teller behind the counter. "I want to go to heaven," she said, kindly receiving the gospel handout. While walking on the trail one day, I saw a man who had a gentle smile, and later we passed each other for a second time. I fumbled for a gospel handout, but my zipped-up rain jacket kept me from quickly pulling one out from my hooded sweatshirt underneath. I rationalized by thinking that was God's sign to pass him without proclaiming the gospel. But the Holy Spirit seemed to nag at me. I said to God, "I really don't want to do this."

I said to God, "I really don't want to do this."

Finally, fully convicted, I spun around and picked up my pace in order to catch up with him on the trail. It took about a quarter mile to finally catch him. He was still smiling and kind enough to receive God's Word. He told me his name was Mark, and I thanked him, wishing him a blessed walk as we parted. Then I prayed that he would read the gospel handout. God frequently allows me to offer His Holy Word by catching up with someone, when I missed an opportunity to gift them with the gospel, forgiving me for my reluctance.

It is not always pleasant when proclaiming the gospel—even painstakingly hard at times, but Oswald Chambers encourages me with his words, " . . .*gracious uncertainty* and *breathless expectation* . . ." [Reference credit: Cathy Wiruth] That often seemed to be what I encounter as I proclaim Jesus. Once there was a young lady who helped me find some items in the grocery store. I thanked her and offered her God's Word. She said, "No, you just go ahead and hang onto it." She did not welcome my offer, but thankfully many people do. On another occasion, I was talking with a friend about something that seemed to be bothering her—I made a general reference to God's sovereignty, to which she responded, "That's bull____!" I was so shocked I didn't know what to say! Then there was the time I dropped off a bill in a mailbox. As I turned around to walk home, I unexpectedly saw a lady sitting on the steps of the nearby building. I asked her, "May I give you some good news?" She said, "Sure." As I drew near to hand her God's Word—the gospel handout, she asked, "What kind of good news is it?" I said, "It's a gift of "Jesus Joy." She looked very disappointed. I said, "You don't seem very excited about it." She shook her head and said something like, "No, I'm not." I said, "I'm sorry—I won't bother you." Disappointed, I said goodbye and walked away. I trust God's providential plan for her and for me. Hopefully, we both willingly receive what He desires to teach us.

One night at the airport we all waited for updates, hoping we would get home. A mechanical malfunction forced a change of planes in another city, and we were delayed several hours. I spoke with a man near the departure gate, Nate, who had one word to say, "Frustrating!" He seemed very discontented. I prayed for guidance from the Holy Spirit. Over a couple hours we spoke casually three or four times as flight updates emerged. As I recall, I asked him if I could share what Jesus had done in my life—his emphatic response was, "I don't believe in it..." I tried to be wise as a serpent, gentle as a dove, loving, relational and patient. With a sense of urgency just before the flight I tried to engender enough courage, offered him the gospel handout and asked him, "May I give you some good news?" With disgust, he quickly responded, "Nope."

I set out on a walking trail toward a pond where wintering geese reside. As I approached the pond, there were three people on the opposite side of the trail by the stream, practicing various tricks with hula hoops, along with music. After watching the geese take flight, I started back home. As I walked by these young people, I waved. The young man waved back, for which I was thankful. After walking a few hundred feet, a theological debate arose within me. I struggled as to whether I should go back and proclaim Jesus. I said to God, "I hate this." (that feeling of wrestling with the conviction that I should go back, take a risk and proclaim the gospel) The last thing in the world I wanted to do at that point was return to them. But the following scripture came to mind, "My grace is sufficient for you, for My power is perfected in weakness." (2 Corinthians 12:9) I prayed, "God, I am powerless and weak." He gave me the courage and strength to go back. I humorously asked the three, "When will the show be ready?" They laughed. We introduced ourselves, and I thanked Daniel for waving back to me. I asked him if he would be kind enough to receive good news. He responded with a smile, "I receive it!" I was so shocked I said, "Wow!" He along with Juanita and Stephanie were so kind to me. Stephanie even apologized for not seeing me wave so she could wave back. I trust they will be exposed to the Word, that God will be glorified, and His good and perfect will shall come out of this faith encounter. The next time this happened on the trail by the same bench along the stream, I didn't hesitate. I stopped immediately. That time, a man named Roger said, "I'm a Christian." He was happy to keep the gospel handout to pass on to someone in need of encouragement and hope. On another walk, I saw a young man I previously greeted, who kindly responded, but looked straight ahead, not making eye contact. Again, I said hello as we passed and again, he responded, friendly but seemingly detached, inwardly focused and again looking straight ahead without making eye contact. I looked back as he continued on, thinking I might catch up with him, but not this time. I regretted not stepping out in faith to briefly give him a gift of the gospel. I continued on the trail and came to a bridge over the stream where a couple stood and enjoyed the beautiful setting. I greeted them and planned to continue walking. I was surprised when the man responded warmly, with a foreign accent. I immediately thought, "I can't do this again." So, I stopped and introduced myself. Bahman and Manija were from Iran. A delightful couple, both with pleasant smiles. I showed them the gospel handout and told them the story about the red heart and cross. Manija asked, "May I have that?" I was so excited when she asked for it. That usually never happens. Then Bahman said, "I don't want to take your last one." So I gave him one as well, and we talked for a few minutes. Before I left, I thanked them for blessing me. It was a *joyful Jesus* [Credit: The Martins] encounter for all of us, though it was mostly God and very little me. My evangelist Brother, Pastor Bruce stated, "By the way, from sales training and life experience, most people will accept or receive something that's handed to them. God continues to look for folks who will hand Him to others." At that time, I was convicted to be deeper in prayer, more discerning, more willing to step out proactively in faith without doubting, trusting the Holy Spirit to lead me. I was low on faith and trust in the character of God, seen in my reluctance to obey. Regarding such reluctance, a friend from Church, Jennifer Szilagyi, stated, "Obedience can sometimes be difficult, but often when it is hardest it is actually sweetest."

On the day my mother-in-law was buried, my brother-in-law, Lee, forgot a shirt when they traveled down to the city from the mountains. He had to go out and quickly buy one, at which time he stopped to get coffee. While there, two police officers waited in line behind him. They asked him how he was doing. "Well, I'm going to bury my Mother today," he said. They tried to comfort him. Lee spoke to them of being encouraged by Jesus that morning, on the radio, Billy Graham, etc. They were quick to agree. The young lady behind the counter overheard their conversation. Her response was, "That is so cool." He told me afterwards that if he had a gospel handout with him, he could have given it to her. One might say this was an example of God's divine appointment—He uses our mistakes! The truth is, you never know who will be impacted when proclaiming the gospel, maybe someone not even part of the conversation who was just meant to hear the message.

> "Obedience can sometimes be difficult, but often when it is hardest it is actually sweetest."
> —Jennifer Szilagyi

The founder of a Christian ministry spoke at our Church many years ago with a message about what he called *The War Of All Wars*—our spiritual battleground. He made a statement regarding God's call to start his ministry, that caught me off guard. He said, "I know it was God's will because I didn't want to do it!"

One day the dreaded morning approached for me to renew my expired driver's license. Concerns mounted in my mind about proof-of-documentation requirements. These included such things as social security number, organ donor, military veteran, long distance vision changes, and marriage license issues, plus people's stories of long waiting lines, ad infinitum. In years past I would be intensely frustrated. But on this occasion, I reluctantly chose to trust God, knowing that He could open doors of ministry during even the most mundane and time consuming of administrative burdens. After much procrastination, I headed to the Driver's License office where I was greeted with friendly smiles and helpful suggestions. Finally, I was called to the counter and sternly asked, "How can I help you?" I asked about the person's smile as their demeanor quickly and kindly warmed. God began to transform the dreaded task into a joyful, worshipful time of blessing, as three people happily received Bible scripture with smiles, and laughter began to spread throughout the office. I praised God for the unexpected "Jesus Joy." On the way home, I stopped at a grocery store where a lady named Donna I previously met, again joyfully received a quantity of gospel handouts to offer customers. I continue praying for her lungs to heal. I was back home much sooner and more greatly blessed than I ever expected! Early the next morning God woke me with the inaudible words, "Don't be bashful," and "...not ashamed of the gospel ..." I went to the study and wrote the following poem:

"Don't be bashful, nor gospel ashamed
Cause downcast souls abound
Loan them your smile or a laugh
Let "Jesus Joy" resound;
Christ's light and life transform our hearts
Where shattered hope cries out
Tears speak loud and anguish soul destroy
As Satan's darkness roams about."

chapter 7
Praying And Planting

About 15 years ago Tim Huegel, a friend from work, was inspired by his daughter to give me a beautiful prayer book for my birthday. It had a hard cover with the 23rd Psalm engraved on the front. This gift was so meaningful to me that it became my prayer journal ever since. It has been a good resource to help keep me grounded in prayer. Sometimes when I reflect on its contents, I see the unpredictable ebb and flow of my life, peaks and valleys, a river of many tears for myself and others—yet a clear picture of God's unfailing provision. Between July and September of 2006, I struggled with a number of personal and work issues. I entered many prayer requests as each issue arose, along with some answered prayer. But as the burden of cumulative prayer needs continued to build, I grew weary. Low on hope, I went back to the July 4, 2006 prayer entries and wrote, "I need God more than I need my problems solved." As important as prayer is, I seemed to discern in my spirit that even though many of my problems may go unresolved, I could not go on without closely and deeply sensing God's presence. This realization began to change the way I prayed—to a balance between petitions and joyful praise. Thankfully, Psalm 50:15 states in part, "and call on me in the day of trouble; I will deliver you, and you will honor me." I was so thankful to God; subsequently He filled me with joy overflowing, the riches of Christ, granting me many answers to my prayers. For several years, I rode the bus to work. During that time, God frequently allowed me to proclaim the gospel, usually through giving people a gospel handout, unless an extended conversation was possible. I wrote their names on a slip of paper, so I could remember to pray for them. Later, I entered their names in my Prayer book when I got home.

Praying before planting the gospel seed is essential for me to be impactful in people's lives through God's Word and the work He is doing. *Jews for Jesus* stated, "The best pre-evangelistic work is prayer. Nothing prepares a heart to receive the gospel like faithfully asking God to work in someone's heart for their good and His glory." (*Jews for Jesus* Newsletter, April 2019) In this dark world, my prayer preparation is essential to planting the seed of the gospel. When my prayer life is lethargic, my witness is weak. And when I fail to trust God, it is even weaker.

One day as I walked toward my regular grocery store, I prayed to God, remorseful about not trusting Him to open a door of ministry, asking Him to forgive me. For some strange reason, I too often think I can do God's work without His power, which of course I cannot. As soon as I finished my prayer, I entered the store, passing a young lady who was exiting. She was pushing a grocery cart and asked if I needed it. "Yes, thank you. Bless you," I answered. The Holy Spirit convicted me to catch her attention. I had about one second to act before she got too far away. I don't remember exactly what I said, but I quickly spoke to her, introduced myself, and asked her name. She said her name was Emily. I offered her a gospel handout, which she was kind enough to receive. She looked at it for a moment, then looked up at me with a smile and said, "Thank you for this!" Emily seemed unusual in her deep appreciation—almost as if she was pondering in her heart, the visual imagery of the cross, and the majestic power and love of God's Word. Then I said goodbye, as we parted, thankful for what God did in that moment. To me, one of God's great gifts is when I give His Word to others, especially when it is unexpected by both them and me!

I need to be bathed in prayer to joyfully proclaim the gospel. I often pray that people will read God's Word after I give them a gospel handout. Oswald Chambers stated, "When the truth is preached, the Spirit of God brings each person face to face with God Himself. The moment we recognize our complete weakness and our dependence upon God will be the very moment that the Spirit of God will exhibit His power." [Credit: Bill Warner devotion]

Many years ago, in the Wednesday morning men's Bible study at our Church, we were encouraged to individually pray later that same day at noon, which came to be known as "High Noon Prayer." [Credit: Tom Hester] To help me remember to deepen my prayer time that day, I often wrote "HNP," for High Noon Prayer, in my calendar, otherwise I would get too busy and forget. God often works in ways unbeknownst to me, and I see His work after the fact. If I earnestly prepare in prayer and obey in trust, I am frequently blessed with mysterious joy to the point of tears. If I am not prepared, I miss the blessings God intended. John 3:8 states, "The wind blows wherever it pleases. You hear its sound, but you cannot tell where it comes from or where it is going. So, it is with everyone born of the Spirit."

As I waited in line at the pharmacy for my prescription, I struck up a conversation with a very pleasant man, waiting for his prescription to be completed. I assumed that I would give him God's Word as I left. But when I turned around to depart, he was gone. I felt sad because it represented a missed opportunity, after we established a good relational connection. In retrospect, I did not ask God what to do. I did not pray. I was not spiritually discerning. When I fail to adequately pray, my sowing is compromised. In this context, *Jews for Jesus* stated, "This may or may not open up a conversation down the line, but whether or not it does, a seed will be planted." (*Jews for Jesus* newsletter, May 2019 p. 4)

One day I prayed to be close to God. John, a believer, encouraged me that day as I offered a gospel handout to him. He said, "Keep on doing what you're doing, even if people don't like it." He spoke of people in reference to going to hell. He said he tells them, "I can give you directions... just keep on doing what you're doing!" Even in persecution, Psalm 126:5 encourages me when I remember the words, "Those who sow with tears will reap with songs of joy." When a ministry door opens for me, (2 Corinthians 2:12) and God allows me to cross paths with someone to share Christ's gospel of peace, my time is often limited to just seconds, or perhaps a minute or two. It is always a blessing when

I have more time, but that is rare. My brother in Christ, Bill Warner, signs off in his daily devotion with, "It's a tough world. Stay prayed up!" If I am prayed up, the Holy Spirit often bestows wonderfully mysterious "Jesus Joy" blessings with spiritually relational conversations. These joyful encounters are often greater than I could ever imagine. One example is when God causes an unsaved person to use keywords in conversation, such as peace, truth, love, purpose, grace—pivotal words that invite transition towards needed spiritual matters. Another example is when God leads them to introduce events in their lives that may point toward pain, loss, disappointment, and grief that only the shed blood of Jesus can heal.

One morning as I walked along a trail, I prayed. I saw in my spirit how Satan accusingly lies to me when people choose not to receive God's written or spoken Holy Word—Satan often seems silent when people do receive it, until he has another opportunity. One morning as I was walking, I waved to an elderly couple walking on a divergent trail, and the lady waved back. I told God I hoped we could cross paths again, although I didn't expect it. About a half hour later God blessed me when I saw them on the trail once again. After meeting Meryl and Gwen, I thanked her for waving, and we engaged in a delightful conversation. I soon discovered that they both had bright, scientific minds with aerospace backgrounds, so I asked them questions about the mysteries of quantum entanglement, black holes and neutron star collisions, of which they knew far more than me. Gwen mentioned that she believed there are stars [elements] in everything. From the branch of a cottonwood tree that Meryl picked up while we talked, they pointed out the perfectly shaped star inside the core of a twig! Gwen began to share her global peace efforts over many years. We talked about reconciliation initiatives between Jewish and Palestinian youth taking place around the world. I was excited in my spirit when the word *peace* entered into our conversation, because I am thankful for the gospel of peace—the Prince of Peace. Gwen even spoke of *grace*. We talked for perhaps 30 minutes. Toward the end of our conversation I briefly testified of Christ in me. Since Gwen was more talkative, I offered her a gospel handout with God's Word alone, which she reluctantly received. She looked at it, then looked at me and said, "I'm retired clergy—I could probably quote all of this to you." I sensed in my spirit her resistance. Mysteriously, when I asked her if she knew someone she could give this to who was without hope, she immediately and emphatically said "No." I was surprised and saddened to hear her say that, and felt a little like the Apostle Paul might have felt when he stated, "Have I now become your enemy by telling you the truth?" (Galatians 4:16) I thanked Meryl and Gwen for our time together. I was grateful to God for allowing the three of us to relate to one another for that long on the trail—yet I went away perplexed. Upon self-examination, did I speak the truth? Did I speak the truth in love? Was I insensitive to her? Did Gwen have some deep soul wounds that were bubbling up to the surface, of which I triggered, or failed to discern? Did I fail to listen to the Holy Spirit? As I walked on, I thanked God, and prayed. I wish I had prayed more during the course of our time together, asking God to prepare good soil for planting the gospel seed of faith in Jesus. I believe my inadequate praying minimized my witness for Christ, and even allowed Satan to steal some of my joy. Sometimes it seems like I get in God's way and contribute to my own painstaking journey.

One morning before entering the grocery store, I made the "mistake" of taking time to pray in the car, and God provided multiple blessings. As I entered the store, I saw Mike, the employee I met three days earlier. I smiled as he passed me, exiting the store. Later, I saw him in the men's restroom where I was placing gospel handouts. We spoke momentarily, and he said he still planned to attend our Church's worship service the next day. Then I was blessed to see a brother in Christ from Church who just survived a serious rollover accident, where he hung from his safety belt before being rescued by workers nearby. He gave our Lord great thanks for watching over him throughout this experience. As I continued shopping, I noticed an elderly lady with a gentle smile. She rode in an electric cart and shopped with her caregiver. I saw her a couple more times and was about to leave the store when I noticed her in the checkout line. I stepped back, gave her a gospel handout, thanked her for her nice smile and asked her name. Her English was broken, and difficult to understand. I bid her goodbye. Her caregiver smiled and thanked me for giving the lady the gospel gift. That evening I was hurrying to get a walk in before dark, and the coming snow. Having no expectations, fortunately I placed gospel handouts in my pocket within a plastic protector and put them into the outside pocket of my jacket, so I could quickly retrieve one if God opened a door.

One morning in December 2017 while in the grocery store parking lot, I prayed, "Heavenly Father, show me where you are working..." I was still in the car with the windows up, when I began hearing someone's car alarm. As I got out of the car and walked toward the store, the alarm grew louder. Then I spotted the car, with the front door open. A young Mother held her baby, talking on her cell phone, obviously in some distress. She was troubled, not knowing how to shut off the alarm. After introducing myself, I tried to put her at ease. She said her name was Summer, and her baby's name was Emmarest. I offered to help, and she agreed. It was a Subaru—I had no idea what to do, but the Holy Spirit led me to pray out loud, "Heavenly Father, I don't know what to do but my eyes are on you. Help me now I pray in Jesus Holy Name, Amen." Summer seemed unappreciative and unimpressed with my prayer. After some questions and pushing a few buttons on the car door, the alarm continued. So, I asked her if I could just sit down in the seat for a moment, put the keys in the ignition, and try a few things. This was risky, being a young mother with an infant, giving her car keys to a complete stranger, and allowing me to sit in her car, behind the steering wheel. I put the keys in the ignition and the alarm stopped. I noticed that her steering wheel was turned at an angle, which was problematic on my car. So, I straightened out the steering wheel and explained how that contributed to the problem. She seemed relieved but withdrawn. I trust that the Lord will work in her heart. After watching what God did following my prayers, how He worked at that moment, and what He perfectly orchestrated in that situation, I asked, "God, are you perfect?" Hopefully a seed of faith was planted by God in Summer's heart.

God answered my prayer as our mission team headed to the airport. We were on a return mission trip back to a densely populated country with severe poverty, a highly restricted country closed to the gospel. Al Johnson, Director of World Outreach at our Church previously asked me if I would prepare a devotion for a Sunday worship service once in that country. I agreed. On the day of our departure, he unexpectedly asked me to ride in his car from Church to the airport.

I soon spoke of one of the first things that was a heavy burden on my heart, "Al, I don't know how to prepare the devotion you've asked me to do, to these people who have nothing." He said, "It is always a good idea to remember the people in Africa who have nothing, but often have more joy than those of us in America who have everything one would ever need." This was a breakthrough for me and served as a turning point in my devotion preparation. This was especially helpful when we visited women in training to become evangelists. I was honored and deeply humbled when asked to pray for them, knowing that there was a risk of them being killed for their faith and courage in Christ. I am reminded of David in Psalm 27:6, "Then my head will be exalted above the enemies who surround me; at his sacred tent I will sacrifice with shouts of joy; I will sing and make music to the Lord." Let us joyfully shout the good news from the rooftops and mountaintops!

When I offer people God's Word through a gospel handout, they respond in a variety of ways. In a Mideastern restaurant, after I paid the bill, I asked the cashier, "How can I pray for you in Jesus name?" Kaisen was shocked! He immediately stated, "Oh, no! Don't pray for me in Jesus name." I didn't fully understand his motives behind that response. We went on to develop a friendship over several years, but he was always convinced that there are errors in the Bible. But in another restaurant, the receptionist Nadine stated after receiving a gospel handout, "That's the best gift I've ever received from a customer." When I asked "Boo" in a different restaurant, "Are you a follower of Jesus?" he said, "I'm undecided right now; open to all." One man said when he looked at the gospel handout "Ah, Genesis."

Unfortunately, God has had to teach me many difficult lessons as I pray and plant the seed of the gospel. A man named Mike laughed at me when I gave him a gospel handout. I try to be a blessing for Jesus to everyone I meet, even if I don't give them a gospel handout—and especially when they reject the gospel message, are reluctant or displeased. As I walked into a store, I received a rather cool greeting from Daniel, who had a stone-sober bearded face. Trying to be cheerful, I asked him, "How is your smile today?" He didn't flinch. In response, his co-worker said, "He doesn't have one." So, I loaned him mine. Daniel was very helpful and as I left, he received a gospel handout and we all had a smile and a laugh together. I prayed that he would read at least one verse. And when a Physician Assistant, who cared for my wife, left our home for the last time, I said I hoped our paths would cross again. I asked her if I would see her in heaven. She said, "I hope so." That reply often saddens me because God's Word clearly states we can know that we will have eternal life. I hope everyone I meet will make a decisive eternal life decision, and not risk eternal condemnation by default. At the grocery store I surprised a young mother I have seen before, with a gift for her son tucked into a gospel handout. But as I slid it onto the counter it kept going, falling on the floor. She had to lean over to pick it up, and I felt awkward about my clumsiness. Then I offered a gospel handout to another employee, which was refused. As I drove home, I felt down and unworthy, on which Satan thrives. I continued praying in the car as I headed for a meeting downtown.

When my wife, Barbie, was in the hospital's acute rehab after her colon surgery, I struck up a conversation in the hallway with a man named William. He was short and skinny and wore a grody old baseball cap with a radical curve in the bill, which I admired! William was very outspoken and quickly opened up with conversation starters, and conversation stoppers! He mentioned how deep the racial problem is in his city. Years ago, I asked God to grant me friendships with more diversity from my own background and race, which He did, so William's statement resonated with me. But I was saddened as William and I talked. He stated that he felt it was "just not fair" that his stepson, who was in his 50s, was suffering with cancer at an early age. In my spirit, I was reminded of Jesus' "unfair" death on the cross. William and his wife had been staying in a motel for about a month because their local relatives were unable to provide a temporary place to stay, and the expense was concerning him. I needed to get back to Barbie, but I felt like I needed to offer him the gospel handout in case our paths never crossed again. As we conversed, I hoped he would be receptive to me as I described the red heart and cross graphic God gave me many years before. William looked at the gospel handout, thought about it, then handed it back. This doesn't happen very often. Usually people will accept it and express appreciation, even if they may throw it away later. I thanked him for considering it, but I wish

I listened more to God, let His Words be my words, and trusted the Holy Spirit to lead our conversation. I felt great compassion for William, as he endured life's burdens, without God's presence in his life. I continued to pray for him after we parted, and asked God to please forgive me if my spiritual pride got in the way of God's work. I wish I would have been more sensitive, discerning and caring toward William rather than feeling as if without him reading the gospel handout, God would not be able to touch his heart and mind. I increased my prayer for him. The next day I unexpectedly saw him in his stepson's hospital room. His stepson was being moved back to oncology, and we were able to exchange a friendly greeting across the rooms from each other. While I waited in the lobby until I could go back and see my wife, William walked out with a young person that looked like she was probably his granddaughter. She called him "Wild Bill." "Used to be," he replied. I was hoping God would give me another chance to connect with him, but that never happened. We need to pray for people in need, even if we don't agree with them, their lifestyle, behavior, and beliefs. It doesn't matter what the differences are, we are all spiritual beggars in God's eyes, since no one is righteous except God alone.

I hate missed opportunities for proclaiming the gospel. Sometimes, when we are open to proclaiming the gospel, God opens doors of opportunity that are highly perishable, especially if we are not prepared. It may be a split second or two that makes the difference; a distance of a couple feet versus several feet; a brief glance toward, versus away. As we approached the red stop light, a Hell's Angels motorcyclist was in the lane next to me on my left, just a few feet away. I had a gospel handout ready in the right seat, which would have only taken a moment, the blink of an eye. I had plenty of time because the light just turned red. I was just ready to open the door, hand it to him with a blessing and get back in the car. Then, I looked into the rear-view mirror and saw two rows of cars behind me. I started thinking, "Is this a safety issue?" I became fearful and hesitant. Mark 5:36 states, in part, "Don't be afraid; just believe." I had the faith, but the fear won out. On the way home I asked God to forgive me for not being active in proclaiming my faith. I regretted not taking action. I wished so much that I had given him a gospel handout. Would it have been a risk? Yes. Would it have been worth the risk? I think so. A few months later, God placed another "motorcycle" ministry opportunity in front of me. Just a couple hundred yards down the street lives a young, high income man, whom I heard is very difficult to approach. I inquired about him one day and was asked, "Haven't you heard?" It turns out that he apparently pulled in front of a speeding motorcyclist, resulting in a broadside crash right by the entrance to our neighborhood. I was saddened to hear this killed the motorcyclist. The crash also totaled this man's pickup and leveled the marquee near the neighborhood entrance. I prayed for him, not knowing what he was going through. I asked God to give me the courage to speak with him, and hopefully encourage him with the hope of Christ. I'd like to share with him how I was saddened to hear about his accident. I hope that he will open up about it, allowing God to introduce healing and restoration. Had it happened to me, I would feel heavy, heartbroken, and numb.

One day as I pulled up to a Christian coffee house ministry where I try to connect with the homeless, I spotted a man partially obscured from full sight, standing near an alley. This isn't the safest part of the city. A person had been killed a year or two before in the apartment right where he was standing. I popped open the trunk and went behind my car to take out peeled and cut apples for the homeless, since they can't eat apples with skin on due to the condition of their teeth—but they can "gum" the inside of the peeled apples. The man looked suspicious to me, as he moved further behind a tall, wooden fence. I tried to monitor his presence out of the corner of my eye, just for my own safety. I felt convicted by the Holy Spirit to offer Bible scripture to him. I prayed to God, "Lord, this could kill me, but then I would be with you." So, I reluctantly walked over and approached him. He seemed spaced out. He wore headsets, so he could not hear my greeting. I handed him the gospel handout; he smiled. He seemed very kind and said he could not hear me because of the music. He seemed happy to receive God's Word, and I was thankful that I took a risk.

I was blessed when my friend from Church, Greg Litten, shared the following story associated with his Dad and his Dad's caregivers. They would say to Greg, "I want to sit down and talk," even if his Dad was not always happy with that. Greg stated, "Be aware of the blessing. They feel like God has abandoned them. I try to weave Christ, through the Holy Spirit, with the perfect message for them, e.g., 'It says in the good book . . .' The good Lord has shown me how to get along with people; shaped me, and it is spilling out; helping them to have joy in the hiccups, heartaches and hurdles of life through which they suffer."

"I am able to nurture them because they are down on themselves; lead them out of darkness in little subtleties; one liners, like his old boss told him, 'You can't go wrong by doing right;' through actions, demonstrating, loving, little tad bits from experiences; the joy of having offered them a *hand up*, not a *handout*." Greg is a humble man of God, a gift to me, a blessing from the Lord. God created a blessed friendship between us that brought me a refreshing, mysterious stream of joy. Greg is one of the miracles God gave me, to pray for me and inspire

> " . . .helping them to have joy in the hiccups, heartaches and hurdles of life through which they suffer."
> —Greg Litten

me to finish this book. To encourage me, Greg, who is an avid snow skier, sent me a card. He drew two skier's paths in the snow, challenging me with one path labeled "never stop turning," and the other "never stop praying." We pray for each other and for our wives.

Praying in the car at the grocery store is some of my best, uninterrupted prayer time with the Lord. This is especially true when it becomes a great source of deep, pre-evangelism preparation. This enables me to hear God's still small voice, His gentle whisper, helping me know with whom to proclaim the gospel. But, sometimes the painstaking journey toward soul winner's joy gets discouraging when I witness for Christ. This is true whenever I am rejected, the gospel is rejected, or I fumble over my own false starts. For example, one day in the grocery store parking lot, I picked up some trash off the pavement just outside my car. I threw it in the trash can just before entering the store. I quickly realized I accidently threw out the gospel handouts in their protective pocket, so I went back to the car to get more. After returning to the store, I placed a small stack of gospel handouts into the upper basket of the grocery cart, and almost immediately they fell through the bars into the main basket. I scooped them up and placed them into the upper basket. Moments later, they fell into the main basket yet again. Embarrassed and frustrated, I picked them up once more, and continued shopping. Then as I was a few feet from the car with a cart load of groceries, a package of grape tomatoes fell to the ground and every tomato was now resting in a muddy pool of water in the parking lot. My wife thought it was funny! As I have gotten older, these things frustrate me more. But that was not as embarrassing as the time several gospel handouts fell on the floor right in front of someone, and I tried to discreetly gather them as if there was nothing to see here. Just before my clumsy moment, God allowed me to offer a gospel handout to a lady in the adjacent checkout line. She looked at me with an expression of surprise and said something like, "Well, aren't you kind." She used the word kind or kindness twice in our conversation, as she thanked me. The comments of other ladies about the red heart and cross graphic, representing the inseparable connection between the cross and love, made perfect sense to her. But the very next day I offered a gospel handout to a lady who said, "I reject that; I'm a Jew." This was really sad to me since they have no true way to atone for their sins apart from the Messiah.

I was saddened even further in a brief conversation with a lady in the neighborhood as I was about to hit the trail. She told me about a space mission, of which she was a part. She told me the name of the program and quickly laid out its goals. Since one of our friends lost her son, who happened to have the same name as this space mission, I hoped this neighbor lady would be willing to pray for her. "Karin, are you a praying woman?" I asked. "Occasionally." Her statement surprised me, and I had no idea how to respond. I'm not even sure I did. Now I pray for her. At least each Christmas, I have the opportunity to bless their home with a small gift containing God's Word. I trust Him.

I offered a gospel handout to a lady in a store who said she was a Christian. She did not want to keep the good news to offer it to anyone else, saying, "It is best for you to keep it." But just as I checked out, the lady behind me in line was very thankful for the gospel handout. It brought joy to her spirit and mine. I still find it a challenge to listen to God's still small voice, His gentle whisper. How do I maintain situational awareness, so I know how, when and where God is working? Paraphrasing, Jesus said in John 5:19, 20, "Show me where you are working so I can see your work and do your work in like manner." I am so thankful that God, in His mercy and grace, knows when I fall short and need to be encouraged. He knows perfectly when to bestow His stored-up goodness (Psalm 31:19) upon me, to help me press on toward the goal. My wife knows I am often short on patience. With God's help I am trying to improve. I discovered if I trust God when I am struggling with patience, He helps me. An example was when I was in a store and I sensed that an employee I asked for help had prematurely dismissed my request. I tried looking to the Lord for guidance to patiently and kindly respond. I have found that frequently, like Jonah, God gives me a second chance. Often when I go back a second time to the same person for help, sometimes apologizing for my confusion, God opens the door to offer His Word—His power through my weakness.

My friend Reggie, a homeless street preacher and a man after God's own heart, said, "I pray, and then I watch things unfold. All His works are good." I asked him one day how I could pray for him. He said, "Patience." Then he said something that caught me off guard. He said he used to pray for patience. He quit praying for patience because every time he did, God would allow some of the most difficult people into his life. So even though he quit praying for patience, he wanted me to ask God to grant him patience. The next time we talked he said difficult people came into his life again, so he asked me to stop praying for patience. He then asked me to pray for God's mercy, grace and favor—Reggie and I both need to be careful what we ask for!

chapter 8
Exuberant "Jesus Joy"

One morning as I prayed the Lord's prayer, I thought I needed to remind myself of the Greek meaning for "hallowed," (holy). Then I wanted to review the words for "heaven." As I studied the meaning of the Greek word for heaven in the context of the Lord's Prayer (ouranois), I found it included sky, happiness, power, and eternity. I was pleasantly surprised, even thrilled when I read the last phrase— "specially, the Gospel." How wonderfully blessed I was to see God's Holy Word connect the words "Heaven" and "Gospel!"

I am so thankful that God progressively sanctifies me (to make holy, purify, consecrate, venerate), often doing a new thing in me (Isaiah 43:19). The way I proclaim Jesus to people now is different than ten years ago, ten months ago and even ten days ago. For example, I just asked a mother of an adopted girl, "Will you allow me to give your daughter a gift from Jesus?" I never used those words before in reference to the gospel handout, but they seemed to just flow naturally, as I was led by the Holy Spirit. They are true words. Jesus is the Giver and the gift, giving His life so that we might have life in Him.

But I often stumble, fumble and bumble applying the gospel—or misapplying the gospel, for better or for worse as the case may be. This contributes to my subsequent painstaking journey of toil toward pure, exuberant "Jesus Joy." This is not happiness based upon circumstances, but true, deep sacred joy in God. I have God's assurance according to Psalm 37:23, 24, "The Lord makes firm the steps of the one who delights in Him; though he may stumble, he will not fall, for the Lord upholds him with His hand." I am sustained by the words of Isaiah 55:11 "so is My word that goes out from My mouth: It will not return to Me empty but will accomplish what I desire and achieve the purpose for which I sent it." Knowing this, I was very blessed when I returned to a store where a pleasant young lady named Jen previously received a gospel handout. She assured me that she read it, so I knew God was at work. As I proclaim Jesus, I know from Luke 1:37, "For no word from God will ever fail." One night I headed to the grocery store in tears, from depression and doubt. I was tired; it was late, dark, Winter, and I expected nothing from God. With gospel handouts in hand I went into the store. Then I watched as God opened one door of ministry after another, when I gave people the gift of His Holy Word. God strengthened me, encouraged me. Again, I realized when I proclaim God's Word on faith, I have the majestic privilege of watching God do the impossible, and tasting the mysterious, exuberant joy of Jesus' heart.

Often grocery stores offer me a triple ministry relational opportunity, proclaiming the gospel, being a blessing to others and receiving prayer requests. A lady at the packaged meat section once said to me, "I need inspiration." Immediately I thought, "What?! You've got to be kidding me, Lord. I can't believe it!" I responded by saying, "I've got the greatest inspiration in the universe. Jesus loves you!" She received a gospel handout, then shared that she meant she was looking for ideas for supper. I would be waiting a very long time before I hear that open of an invitation again. Only Jesus can meet our deepest needs. On another day at a grocery store, while the person at the cash register was busy scanning items, I looked up and saw a tall, large man whose job it was to place my items back into the cart. I offered him the gospel handout. He stared at it for a second or two. Then a grin from ear to ear appeared on his face, as if he won the lottery! I'm not sure I have ever seen such joy on a man's face before.

One evening near dusk I was walking on the trail near my home, when I came upon a young lady named Jen. She was walking to or from her work. After I offered her a gospel handout, she began to share part of her life. She confessed that she would harm herself [cutting]. I don't remember all of our conversation, but before we parted, I prayed with her. For comfort, she reached out with both of her hands, which I held as we prayed. I followed up with her a number of times. The last I heard from her, she stated that she was doing great and that her life was totally turned around. She seemed very happy and content. I hope she is secure in Jesus. On a separate occasion, one late afternoon I spotted a man underneath his car trying to repair it, while parked in the grocery store parking lot. I was hopeful we could connect about Jesus, so I introduced myself, at which time he slid out from under the car. In the following years I have seen him numerous times, once in prison. Unfortunately, we have since lost contact.

There was another time God decided to use the simplicity of a grocery store parking lot to mysteriously connect me with a man named Wayne. I was in a rush to get home with groceries before Barbie's brother and sister-in-law arrived. Wayne's big silver Ram truck had an intricate black aftermarket storage rack mounted over the top of the cab—it was impressive. He was parked so close to my car that it was tight getting the grocery cart near the car door so I could load up my groceries. Once Wayne arrived, I found myself asking him about the truck and rack. He took great effort to explain all about how he and his Dad used the rack to mount a fishing boat they used for their fishing boat business. I think they led people on fishing trip expeditions. It was very clear that he greatly respected his Dad who served in the Army and made sure to point out his Dad's "special forces" license plate on the truck. God seemed to create a bond of friendship in a moment. I felt pressure to get home, since my wife is dependent on me when her caregiver is not present. But God's work seemed to be a high priority at that moment. So, we continued to talk. He offered to help put my groceries in the car, and to take the cart back, which I appreciated. We shook hands numerous times as I prepared to leave. God wanted a firm connection before we parted. It was then that I proclaimed a deeply complex evangelical message to him; "Jesus loves you very much!" He thanked me for not "being pushy," and told me about all the religions he studied—that he was not an atheist, but that he was an agnostic. I showed him the heart and cross graphic God gave me decades before, and that one woman referred to it as, "Love and the cross are one and the same." I told him the verses were from the Bible, not any of my words. He mentioned the word "Christianity" and was smiling, when he told me he would read the scripture verses. We both agreed it would be a blessing if we saw each other again. I left for home feeling the pressure of being late. Upon my arrival, I discovered that her brother and sister-in-law came early. My wife seemed upset but said nothing. Hopefully, God exchanged my late arrival with His priceless gift of eternal salvation to Wayne. He seemed to be powerfully attracted to God's spoken word by me, as well as God's written Word and living Word, Jesus Christ. Hopefully he was not misdirected by any of my inadequacies.

Once at the grocery store, I greeted a young lady with a friendly smile, and she smiled back. I thanked her for her smile and blessed her with a gospel handout. She looked at it, smiled, and thanked me. Bryan, a store employee, smiled and said, "I always appreciate it when you offer that." [the gospel handout] "I've got more right here. Would you like some to give to others?" I said. I was blessed when he happily received more.

Unless the Holy Spirit convicts me otherwise, I greet people with a smile to encourage them. If they don't have a smile, I try to give them mine, elicit one out of them, convince them they have a great one, or whatever it takes to spread "Jesus joy" to the world. One day I walked up to the grocery store customer service counter, because just before leaving the store I discovered an extra food item at the bottom of my cart which was overlooked at checkout. Realizing that I had not paid for it, I wanted to make it right. When it was my turn, I walked up to customer service and greeted the man behind the counter with a smile, but he returned a harsh, "What do you need?" Suddenly my smile disappeared, and I felt insulted by his rude mannerism. I then told him why I was there, and he assigned a young lady to take my payment for the spinach. Katy was a beautiful young lady with a warm smile. We talked while she processed my payment. It turned out that she was a Christian, and about to begin a "gap year" after high school to go on a mission trip to Poland. "Katy, will do me a big favor?" I asked. "Sure." "Will you please loan your radiant smile to that young man over there?" She quickly called to him and told him what she was doing. He didn't seem to appreciate it, and he didn't smile. I was sad that it ended that way. I felt like I failed to represent the joy of Jesus. I hope to handle it better next time, with God's help. The young man may have been struggling with any number of serious life issues, perhaps I could have been more discerning about this situation.

As I prepared to hit the trail one day, I took four gospel handouts with me. Just as I was about to enter the trail, I saw a lady approaching and the Holy Spirit led me to offer her God's Word. I was stunned as we fellowshipped together, trying to grasp the mysterious way God was working. Her name was Marie-Annick, a joyful French Roman Catholic Christian—as fervent a follower of Jesus as you might care to meet. She was visiting from thousands of miles away. She smiled as she received the gospel handout. I asked her what the red heart and cross graphic meant to her. She responded with a single word, "Love." We deeply discussed our common faith in Jesus, and even some secondary theological differences in our understanding of the Lord. Then we prayed together as Jesus blessed us. I thanked her for blessing me, and later thanked God for His work of grace. As I continued on my walk, I meditated on what God did and was joyful in my spirit, envisioning vividly a small glimpse of what true unity in the body of Christ could look like. As believers, we are all one in Christ Jesus (Galatians 3:28). Later that discussion prompted me to give further thought and study in the areas of venerating, worshipping, original sin, personal sin, under and over emphasis on liturgy, and *mystery surrounded by grace* (her words). Further down the trail, Cory and Mimi blessed me when they received and thanked me for God's Word. But a lady named Wendy received the gospel handout, stating, ". . .some scripture quotes in the Bible I don't agree with . . ." Then Mariam at the grocery store checkout counter, even after a nice conversation, was not real pleased when I offered her good news, receiving it reluctantly. This spectrum of responses represents gospel encounters I experienced on the street and in the marketplace—examples of how God used me in practical, real world everyday circumstances to proclaim Jesus. These relational encounters demonstrate a mysterious, often counterintuitive paradox and joyful irony—God, on faith, seemingly advances His Word and work through us as we testify and bear witness to the gospel, despite suffering along the *path of persecution*. [Credit: Todd Neddleton, VOM] The next day, God's providential intervention through Marie-Annick seemed to become even more clear as I studied Acts 1:14, 2:1, 42,

44, 47—note the presence of praise, joy and salvation; John 17:23; Ephesians 4:4, 13; Colossians 3:14; Hebrews 10:25; and Revelation 19:17. It reminded me in some ways of Luke 1:44, "As soon as the sound of your greeting reached my ears, the baby in my womb leaped for joy." I exchanged "baby in my womb," with "Holy Spirit in my heart," because I was obviously not pregnant.

One day in a doctor's waiting room, I saw Tedra, a young lady I met on a previous occasion. During our first meeting, I gave her a gospel handout. But this time, I did not recall our earlier meeting, so I offered her another gospel handout. She said, "I actually have it by my bedside, but I'll take another one." Then I asked Lindsey close to her, "Did I give you one before?" She said, "Yes, I keep it in my locker." While in the waiting room, a lady was reading the newspaper. I asked, "Is there any good news in there?" "No," she said and was kind enough to receive the good news of God's Word. During this same time period, God blessed me over several days with more opportunities to proclaim His Word. At a shoe store, Evan thanked me for the gospel handout and stated, "I really appreciate that." Then a young man named Zach and I spoke about God's Word—what a blessed encounter. As I offered a young man named Josh a gospel handout, I asked, "May I bless you?" "It's never a bad day for a bless!" Josh replied when he accepted it. I never heard anyone say that before! One person upon receiving the gospel handout said it will, "Get me through the week!" Another gentleman said, "We all need blessings, right? Absolutely!" Sheryl, with a joyful smile, was happy to receive the gospel handout. And unexpectedly in the grocery store, I couldn't help but overhear a young man on his cellphone loudly repeat in frustration, "I can't figure it out," concerning some reduction in his salary. As we talked, he was nice with a friendly smile. He kindly received God's Word and acknowledged that he was seeking the "spirit" for resolution. I cannot express how great a joy and blessing it is for me, whenever I try to bless others with the joy that only God can give.

However, if we don't proclaim the gospel when God shows us where He is working, it often comes at great cost. We can miss being a part of God's Kingdom of heaven work, along with missing His exuberant "Jesus Joy." Spreading the gospel is often a multiplier of our joy, the mysterious correlation between proclaiming the gospel and God's deep, sacred joy.

God often gives me victory when I am fearful in my witnessing, especially with doctors, whom I've come to understand desperately need Jesus just like everyone else! Many doctors have not been pleased with me when I offer the gospel handout to them. But in reference to a chronic problem for which Dr. Loyd treated me, I asked, "Would you agree that we can't resolve this without God's help?" After a brief hesitation, she emphatically said, "Yes!" I asked another doctor, Dr. Carmichael, who greatly helped me, if he attributed the source of his skill as being from God. He was quick to acknowledge God's sovereignty in his life, his role as an agent of God, and that truth transforms. Then he surprised me when he said, "There are no vacancies in the Trinity!" I had to think about that for a minute!

Spreading the gospel is often a multiplier of our joy.

Then there was the time in a grocery store when a lady named Monica pushed her grocery cart slowly behind me in the crowded area near the checkout counter. She kindly apologized for having to squeeze through. Her voice sounded as if she had a deep congestion in her lungs. I introduced myself as we waited in line and told her I hoped her congestion would improve. She told me she was a smoker. Since she had a European name, I asked her about her nationality, and she mentioned numerous bloodlines. As the dynamics of the conversation shifted, I offered her a gospel handout, which she kindly received and said, "Thank you. That made my day!" She moved to another checkout lane that opened up, and I noticed that she was looking at the handout. From across the checkout lane, she said, "I love it!" I was hopeful that at least I could tell her I enjoyed meeting her when she left the store. To my surprise, as I checked out, she came up to me after she finished in the adjacent line and asked, "Can I give you a hug? Can I give you a heart hug?" The cashier who was helping me, smiled as she was right in the middle of the exchange of conversations. I was so thankful that Monica was exposed to God's Word. I believe He intended to bless all three of us with the exuberant "Jesus Joy" of Christ's love, in that moment.

I met a kind man named James at a grocery store where part of his job included rounding up shopping carts in the parking lot. One day he hollered at me as I left the store, commenting about gospel handouts that I selectively place in shopping carts. As we talked, he said, "My manager doesn't like it, but I didn't tell who its coming from. It remains a mystery to him. A little mystery in life never hurt anybody." I needed to be more spiritually discerning and pray for God's guidance in this situation. Over time we have become more like friends, and we joke about him having to pick up the gospel messages out of the carts. But I believe he understands this is a small, important part of God's work.

I was not expecting to see God working on this quick trip to the post office and grocery store. However, in the grocery store I passed two young ladies who looked like they might be sisters, and they were. I don't know or remember why I walked up and offered the gospel handout to them. Lisa and Laura were immediately so delightfully thankful. As it turned out, they were believers. We had a brief greeting as I explained about the lady who described the red heart and cross graphic as, "Love and the cross are one and the same." Lisa responded, "Without the cross, there would be no love!" We all three went away joyfully blessed and encouraged.

One morning after Bible study at Church, a brother in Christ asked me if I would like to join him and others for breakfast in a nearby restaurant. I was blessed by the invitation and a brief chance encounter. Shortly after I arrived, I was greeted by the hostess and so I offered her good news—God's Word. It turned out that she was a believer, named Michelle. When I asked her how I could pray for her she responded, "That I will never lose sight of Jesus." Wise words I never forgot, and a prayer for every believer.

Dr. Robert B. Dallenbach stated, "Jesus is love and that's why we share him." (Paraphrased—February 13, 2019 radio broadcast excerpt, Pillar of Fire, KPOF, Point of Faith 91, *Sharing Jesus*, from Ephesians 1) It is important for me when proclaiming the gospel, to remember that faith expresses itself through love (Galatians 5:6). I need to proclaim Jesus out of sincere love (Romans 12:9). If my love is sincere when I proclaim the gospel, my witness tends to be more discerning and exuberant. If I truly love the Lord, then serving Him, obeying

Him, and proclaiming Him flows naturally as the Holy Spirit leads me. Pastor Timothy Keller stated, "Of course, we share the gospel and evangelize, but only as a means to the end of loving them." (*Galatians For You*, p. 177, in the context of Galatians 6:8-10)

Years ago, when I took the bus to and from work, it was a very encouraging outreach time for me, although there were times that tested me. For example, there was a man who was a constant thorn in my side. I knew every day would be another spiritual battle. One day I found one of my gospel handouts on the floor of the bus. When I picked it up, I saw "Mc @$$hole," handwritten across the cover. I can't say for certain it was the same man, but he always resisted what I was doing. However, there were those moments that made it all worthwhile. Like the time when a man spoke with me after I got off the bus. He knew I placed gospel handouts on the seats and gave them to people on the bus. He asked if I had any extra because he wanted some, which I was thankful to provide. Joshua 1:9 states, "Have I not commanded you? Be strong and courageous. Do not be terrified; do not be discouraged, for the LORD your God will be with you wherever you go." I'm not a great man; just a man. I am humbled when I read, "It does not take a great man to make a good witness," which Bruce Alexander Balmain, 1831 - 1899, stated in his book *The Training of the Twelve*, p. 38.

> "It does not take a great man to make a good witness."
> —Bruce Alexander Balmain.

I am often shocked by people's response when I share God's Word. Especially because, I usually say something as simple as, "Thank you for blessing me with your smile; may I bless you?" at which time I offer them a gospel handout. In a grocery store I received an unexpected triple blessing when I offered three gospel handouts to people, all within mere moments of each other. The first person was a believer in Jesus. She pointed to her heart and said, "You never know where people are—we never know what's in there."

Then the next person to receive the gospel was a lady who just moved here because her company's world headquarters relocated. She said, "Thank you. I needed that; a friend just died unexpectedly." She kept the handout for someone in need in the family of the deceased. And then Toni, the cashier at checkout said, "Thanks, I need that on many days!" It helped remind me that I need to be ready when God opens a faith door of ministry, because people's eternal destiny is at stake.

She pointed to her heart and said, "You never know where people are—we never know what's in there."
—unknown

In 2010, I struck up a conversation in a hospital with a man named Jim, whom I just met in a hallway. I offered him a gospel handout, and we began to talk. He asked, "Have you ever had one of those days? I was going to go to Montana for euthanasia." As we continued to talk throughout this "chance" encounter, I watched God lovingly begin to uplift Jim's spirit and restore his soul—God's divine appointment! When it comes to divine appointments, I will never forget what my dental hygienist and sister in Christ, Missy, once said to me, "Miracles happen every day. If we are not paying attention, we'll miss them. Some people try to explain them away as a coincidence; but I don't think there is such a thing as a coincidence."

I headed downtown one day to meet with my investment advisor and friend, Abiye. But I was spiritually unprepared when I drove up to the parking lot attendant. As I got out, I realized I didn't have a gospel handout ready to give him, and I wasn't carrying any unfolded handouts in my pocket. In fact, I was completely spiritually unprepared. I hadn't prayed, and my short testimony was rusty, if given a chance to share. As I entered the hotel/office building, I found two folded gospel handouts in my billfold, one of which I offered to the hotel receptionist. Before arriving, I usually double check the names of employees I have previously offered a gospel handout. This time, I forgot. I was embarrassed to ask the receptionist her name again. As Christ's ambassador, I believe the least I can do is know their name, because He loves them and knows them by name. After completing my business with Joseph, which he pronounced "Yoseph," I said, "May I ask you a personal question?" He nodded. "Yoseph, do you happen to be Jewish?" I asked, in a caring and respectful manner. "I'm an agnostic, and so are my parents," he replied. I thought we might have a brief discussion about the distinction between trying to follow the divine moral law and following Jesus, but time did not allow, probably by God's design. I could have just briefly offered my testimony, but that didn't occur to me at the moment. Joseph was a very kind, handsome and highly competent young man. He was happy and gracious enough to receive the good news in the form of a gospel handout. We had a good conversation, and after leaving our meeting I silently prayed for his salvation and that he would read God's Word. As I departed the building, I grabbed a gospel handout in the car for the attendant I first met when I arrived. He kindly received it after a momentary hesitation, not being sure of what I was offering him.

I am spiritually unprepared more times than I care to admit. Yet, in God's mercy, He can always make a way for us. Despite my flawed witness, God opened a door within just minutes to proclaim His Holy Word with Jack, Adam, Janai and then Tom, an elderly man who described to me two near death experiences on his bicycle. After we spoke, I wanted to offer my testimony to him, but I waited too long. Pastor Timothy Keller stated, "If we leave out our testimony, it also gives an incomplete picture of how complete Christian fulfillment is. Christ not only appeals to our minds; He fills our hearts." (*Galatians For You*, p. 35)

As I thought a lot about spreading the gospel, it led me to be thankful for theologian Dave Buschart, and his teaching, including the theme of "Both/and" vs "Either/or." On the subject of God's presence, he addressed the question of whether some people may sense God's presence as distant, and some may sense God's presence as near, at different times—so it can be "both/and," not just "either/or." In continuing this thematic thought process, God allows both suffering, and He heals; He is a God of love and justice; Jesus is both human and divine; and we are both material and non-material. In like manner, this leads to the "both/and" of material ministry, and spiritual ministry (life essentials, including the gospel). For example, in Acts 19, Paul both witnessed and cured the sick/cast out evil spirits. And Jesus perfectly mastered both spiritual and material ministry, through which God can miraculously multiply the impact on unsaved lives—one tends to reinforce the other, sometimes simultaneously, sometimes not.

This "both/and" theme helped reinforce our testimony for Christ. A case in point was made for "both/and" spiritual and material ministry in Luke 9:2, "and

He sent them out to proclaim the kingdom of God and to heal the sick." In the context of Acts 6:1-7, author Leslie B. Flynn stated, ". . .Stephen and Philip not only performed their ministry of mercy with the poor, but they also spearheaded aggressive evangelism." (*The Other Twelve*, p. 145) And Flynn reinforced exuberant "Jesus Joy," stating in part, "In both the public city witness and in the private desert evangelism, the message was the same. Philip preached Jesus Christ." "In both settings joy abounded: the city had great joy (Acts 8:8), and the Ethiopian went on his way rejoicing (Acts 8:39)." (p. 151) And in the context of the disciples being with Jesus, excerpts from Robert E. Coleman stated, "One must not overlook that even while Jesus was ministering to others,...Whether He addressed the multitudes that pressed on Him, conversed with the Scribes and Pharisees which sought to ensnare Him, or spoke to some lonely beggar along the road...In this manner, Jesus' time was paying double dividends. Without neglecting His regular ministry to those in need, He maintained a constant ministry to His disciples..." (*The Master Plan of Evangelism*, pp. 45, 46) We need to *live out* the gospel [Credit: Pastor Joe Lloyd] and proclaim the gospel.

Continuing the "both/and" theme, "L.G.," a missionary to Africa stated, "It has long been on my heart to care for missionaries. During the years I have spent in the world of missions, God has opened my eyes to the need to care for these people who have given up much and moved to foreign lands in order to share the Gospel *and* meet the needs of hurting people." To me, this is a beautiful example of God's children involved in both spiritual ministry and material ministry— "both/and," often in seamless harmony.

Spiritual ministry and material ministry— "both/and," often in seamless harmony.

The Bible states in 2 Timothy 4:5, "But you, keep your head in all situations, endure hardship, do the work of an evangelist, discharge all the duties of your ministry." And the Apostle Paul, in an excerpt from Acts 14:22, in context of preaching the gospel, states in part, "We must endure many hardships to enter the kingdom of God,..." Jesus called me to do the sometimes-painstaking hard work of the gospel, knowing it ultimately leads to eternal joy, even if it costs me my life.

Like Joshua, I need to be strong and courageous. Author J.I. Packer stated in the context of Daniel, "Those who know God show great boldness for God." (*Knowing God*, p. 25) Wherever our life circumstances find us, we are commanded by Jesus to go and bear gospel fruit in season and out of season—good fruit that will last. Philippians 1:4-5 states, "In all my prayers for all of you, I always pray with joy because of your partnership in the gospel from the first day until now." Christ's love compelled Paul to the ministry of reconciliation (2 Corinthians 5), reconciling the world to God in Christ, not counting people's sins against them.

> Jesus called me to do the sometimes-painstaking hard work of the gospel, knowing it ultimately leads to eternal joy, even if it costs me my life.

Sometimes brothers and sisters in Christ encourage me to press on proclaiming the gospel, when I hear their stories—such was the case with Emerson, a missionary friend and former addict. He was encouraged by his wife and others to stop being in relationship with a friend of his, who broke into Emerson's Dad's house and stole firearms. Emerson told his wife and others, "We're just going to have to agree to disagree." Emerson's friend angered him because of his actions, but in Emerson's state of addiction, he determined that he needed to fight him to forgive him! Many years later, Emerson's friend telephoned him, after going into a convenience store. Upon entering and leaving the store, his friend ignored a homeless man needing help, when he actually had change in his pocket available. His friend was in tears and despair. He said a voice told him he should have helped the man. Emerson responded, "That voice was the Holy Spirit." This led to Emerson's joy and ultimately his friend's salvation. Emerson said, "To know that another has the possibility of finding the life I have found in Christ, is joyful." And then he added, "This is my best example of loving my enemies."

In reference to Emerson speaking of the Holy Spirit above, he shared about his preparation in deploying as a missionary. As he toiled in all his "doing," he sensed the Holy Spirit's gentle whisper, "Watch what's going to happen!" God blessed Emerson, his wife, my wife and me, joyfully matching up *their* needs and *our* needs in *His* perfect timing in several ways—just as they prepared to proclaim the gospel and make disciples (learners, pupils) in a distant land opposed to Christ.

On one occasion in a grocery store, I offered the good news of Jesus to Perry, a cashier—he sternly and stoically stated, "No thank you!" I was discouraged as I left and began to question in my heart what just happened. Then God mysteriously uplifted me outside the store through two believers who saw what happened. I was so surprised; I was speechless for a moment. I said, "Well, ah, ya know—I'm praying for his salvation." I had no idea where they were at the time I offered the gospel handout to Perry. I don't think they were angels, but I am so thankful for God's loving kindness to me in my time of need.

Missionary Nate Saint reminded us, "People who do not know the Lord ask why in the world we waste our lives as missionaries. They forget that they too are expending their lives... and when the bubble has burst, they will have nothing of eternal significance to show for the years they have wasted." The Apostle Paul joyfully expended himself to the Corinthians, as stated in 2 Corinthians 12:15 in part, "So I will very gladly spend for you everything I have and expend myself as well." Expending myself for Christ is the desire of my heart—just like my homeless friend Reggie, who stated, "Living for the Lord brings me joy. Joy fulfills. Pleasure doesn't last very long." I once read about a young lady [name and source unrecalled] who boldly proclaimed the gospel, stating that she tells unbelievers, "Christianity is more than just being good." She said about her ministry, "Yes, Jesus died. I could have recited that at the age of 2. But Jesus died because the wages of sin is death. There is a penalty that needs to be paid," emphasizing the p's in "penalty" and "paid." Just as the wise men gave gifts to Jesus, we need to give the gift of Jesus to unwise men.

> Just as the wise men gave gifts to Jesus, we need to give the gift of Jesus to unwise men.

As believers, God called us to bear witness to the Holy Name of Jesus, the Christ, testifying about the gospel of peace in our lives. Our *method* is the person of Jesus Christ. Robert Coleman stated, "He was His method." (*The Master*

Plan of Evangelism, p. 74.) We want better methods, but God wants better men. [Credit: Henry Blackaby] When God ordains an open door through the relational ministry of Jesus, it might be for a period of many years, or perhaps just for two minutes or even just two seconds—often *moment by moment* [Credit: C.S. Lewis], as the Holy Spirit leads. I never know what God is going to do, which is why I need to be prayed up—ready (Matthew 24:44), watching and listening for Him. As ships passing in the night, I often proclaim the gospel with others as I hand them God's Word in the form of a gospel handout in about two seconds, sometimes engaging them with a smile and eye contact, perhaps saying something like:

"May I give you a gift of "Jesus Joy?"

"I have a "Jesus Joy" gift for you."

"Will you allow me to give you good news?"

"May I bless you with good news?"

"May I give you a gift of good news?"

"May I give you a gift from Jesus?"

"Jesus loves you *so* much."

"Jesus died for our sins."

"Jesus is of first importance."

"Jesus saved my life."

We don't need to worry about what to say, because when we pray, the Holy Spirit intercedes for us. If God gives me two minutes with someone, I may testify something like, "Will you allow me to tell you the good news of what Jesus did in my life? When I was in college, I was often depressed, especially on Sunday nights, facing another week of meaninglessness. I had no peace, purpose, or power to stop sinning. Years later my first wife was near death, my business was failing, and our young daughter Angie placed a car key into an electric outlet, causing an explosion of sparks! At that precise moment, God 'shocked' me into the realization that my life was going down a dead-end road. I was convicted of guilt in regard to sin, righteousness and judgement. After a two-year Bible study, I received Christ as my Savior, by God's grace through faith in Jesus, giving me peace in my spirit, freedom from the bondage of sin, and the joy and assurance of eternal life in God's presence. Would you like to receive Christ as your Savior?" Romans 12:21 states, "Do not be overcome by evil, but overcome evil with good." God offers us exuberant "Jesus Joy" when we witness to everyday people in everyday places, where He plants us—the best place to do His work.

My brother, Pastor Bruce often asks permission to share his story—his witness in about one minute, as follows, "There was a time in my life when I was angry, lonely and worried about my future. Then one day a friend explained how I could have a relationship with God through faith in Jesus Christ. But I knew how I was living and didn't think God would want any part of me. But my friend explained how much Jesus loved me—that He left a perfect home in heaven with His loving Father to come to a fallen world and broken people to live His life and give His life to pay the price for my sin. When I realized what Jesus had done for me, I asked Him into my heart. Over time He took my anger and gave me His peace. He took my loneliness and gave me His presence. Over time I felt I could trust Him for my future rather than worrying about all the things of which I was concerned. If I hadn't asked Christ into my heart at that time I don't know if I'd be alive today because of how I was living and the choices I was making. The same Jesus who lives in my heart loves you very, very much."

Bruce shared about a conversation with a well-known, prominent couple. The wife said, "We have people to wave to...but no friends." Her husband said to Bruce again, "I think you're my best friend." Bruce shared that the amount of loneliness out there really concerns him. The husband then also asked him again, why he changed from being a drinker/partier to doing what he's doing. Bruce answered, "Jesus messed with me—you can blame Him." He said, "You told me that before." Bruce responded, "It's still true." Bruce's goal is not to force conversation or press for a decision but just to grow their relationship.

My wife, Barbie, sent the following letter September 14, 2019 to a 92-year-old woman who is without Jesus:

Dear Miriam,

It was wonderful seeing you at Jane's memorial service. As I recalled the fond memories of years gone by, I realized how little time we have left of this life. Consequently, because I care for you, I wanted to send you an invitation.

When this life is over and we die, we don't just cease to exist. We, by our own choice, either live with God and His blessings for eternity, or we live separated from God and His blessings for eternity. God is not angry. Instead, He tenderly desires everyone to consciously choose to be with Him for eternity. But, not choosing Him, consciously or unconsciously, is a choice; by not making a choice, a person has already chosen eternity without God. All people have until the moment they draw their last breath to decide but waiting can be very unwise.

God provided a way for us to have hope. That hope comes through the forgiveness of all our sins and reconciliation with God through His Son's death and resurrection. I'm not talking about religion, but a mended relationship with God by believing in His plan for freeing us and giving us hope through Jesus.

Living a good life will not get you into heaven. Being a good person will not get you into heaven. Ignoring the choice that must be made does not make the choice go away. God is loving and wants you to spend eternity with Him. He only requires one thing...that you accept that you are unworthy of His great gift of hope and forgiveness through Jesus.

Right now, you can say, "God, I don't understand all this, but I know I've sinned, I've lived my life without You, and I want to change that right now. I believe that you made one way, through your Son Jesus, for me to be new, have hope and live with you, in joy, forever."

You are precious to God and to me. I pray that we'll spend eternity together.

Love,

Barbie Christian [Deleted]

"Whoever has the Son has life; whoever does not have the Son of God does not have life." (1 John 5:12)

chapter 9
God's Double Correction

For many years, I prayed, "Heavenly Father, I ask you to allow me to serve your Holy Name." When the Apostle Paul, James and Simon Peter identify themselves as a servant, they used a certain Greek word for servant, *doulos* meaning a bondservant, servant, or slave. One of the ways God answered my long standing prayer to serve Him has been by helping me better learn to proclaim the gospel through a coffeehouse ministry that remembers the poor (Galatians 2:10), the oppressed (Isaiah 58), and people of low position (Romans 12:16)—a place where the homeless can hang out with one another. Mysteriously, one way God seemed to call me was to people who have no place to call home. Many of these people live on the street, under bridges, along the river, under trees, in alleys, etc. John Hicks, founder of the ministry over 40 years ago, originally said to me, "Why don't you just come down and hang?" I didn't know what it meant to hang with the homeless.

The coffeehouse has been a source of great spiritual blessing for me, usually with quiet fellowship. It's a peaceful place with an occasional surprise here and there, a little smelly, and a little smoky. There you will find personalities with intense emotions often exacerbated by mental illness and addiction, yet, a safe place for the homeless to "take a leak and take a shower." One of the most impactful ways God often humbles me and corrects me is by learning to love the poor (Matthew 5, Acts 10:31, Galatians 2:10). This helps keep me spiritually grounded [Credit: Lois Johnston], established in Christ and dependent upon

Him. And it provides me with a base of spiritual support to better proclaim the gospel. Ryan Taylor, coffeehouse Director, helped me understand in a spiritual sense, we are all poor beggars—totally dependent upon God for our lives. Jean Vanier stated, in part, "People may come to our communities because they want to serve the poor; they will only stay once they have discovered that they themselves are the poor."

> "People may come to our communities because they want to serve the poor; they will only stay once they have discovered that they themselves are the poor."
> —Jean Vanier

I had a lot to learn so I could love the poor with tender mercy, as Jesus did. I didn't know how to relate to them. Henri Nouwen stated, "When we have discovered God in our own poverty, we will lose our fear of the poor and go to them to meet God." Proclaiming the gospel with the poor helped humble me, since I don't naturally choose to think of myself as poor, but God states in Psalm 86:1-4, "Hear me, Lord, and answer me, for I am poor and needy. Guard my life, for I am faithful to you; save your servant who trusts in you. You are my God; have mercy on me, Lord, for I call to you all day long. Bring joy to your servant, Lord, for I put my trust in you." This was written by King David, and who considers a king to be poor?

As God leads me, I need to love and care for the poor and homeless, because they too are made in His image. Some may *choose* to live on the streets, others may have had it thrust upon them due to the consequences of sin, or perhaps through harsh life circumstances. I see God working, as He calls even poor and homeless believers to serve and minister to those on the street who are without hope and faith, and especially to those who feel like God is not *for* them or has abandoned them. But our covenant-keeping Immanuel—God with us, has not abandoned them. He will never leave them nor forsake them, just as He will not abandon you or me.

Humility plays an important role as I proclaim the gospel so God can use my testimony—I need His wisdom in my witness constantly. In Acts 20:19, Paul stated in part, "I served the Lord with great humility..." Ephesians 3:7, 8, states,

"I became a servant of this gospel by the gift of God's grace given me through the working of His power. Although I am less than the least of all the Lord's people, this grace was given me: to preach to the Gentiles the boundless riches of Christ . . ." God's Holy Word clearly establishes a correlation between humility and preaching the gospel. I can't proclaim the gospel without humility—because James 4:6 states in part, "God opposes the proud, but shows favor to the humble." Pastor John Piper worked at being humble. A few of the ways he and his staff tried to stay humble include, "Prayer—pleading with God for humility—really is crucial...The truth is that I'm a sinner. I wasn't only a sinner. I am a sinner... be more amazed that you're saved than that they're lost." (Referenced in *The Gospel Coalition*, *How to Pursue Humility*, April 30, 2008 discussing John's edited audio transcript entitled *How Do You Remain Humble?*) Additionally, Elisabeth Elliot, reminded us from Deuteronomy 8:2, "Remember how the Lord your God led you all the way in the wilderness these forty years, to humble and test you in order to know what was in your heart, whether or not you would keep His commands."

Whether we are on the street or in the executive suite, we all need Jesus. Without Jesus, it doesn't matter whether we are down and out or up and out, we are still on the outside, looking in. Even when we are materially blessed by God, we need to be humble. My friend Nancy Buschart once said, "humiliation precedes humility." Lord, please humble me and keep me from *spiritual pride* [Credit: Cathy Wiruth], so I am malleable and usable by God, *the way of humility—the way of Jesus.* [Credit: Pastor Emmanuel Engulu] Philippians 2:3 states, "Do nothing out of selfish ambition or vain conceit, but in humility consider others better than yourselves." Whenever I am prideful, I become insensitive, lacking compassion, and my witness for Christ is compromised.

Once I looked at a man sitting among some homeless people, as the Holy Spirit convicted me to walk over to the table and try to connect with him. He introduced himself as "Sandman," his street name—I found out later that his given name was Sandy. He seemed downcast, with his head bowed toward the tabletop. He said to me, "I walk the streets; nobody knows me; they think I'm a bum." The Holy Spirit convicted me to sit down and listen to him, so I "hung" with

Sandman. He poured out his heart in tears, depressed, despondent, speaking of darkness, and mistakes he made. He said his ex-wife was streetsmart; when his children wanted to see him, she knew how to find him. He lived on the street, struggling with horrifying memories of having to kill children carrying bombs on their backpacks in a war-torn country. "All the counselors in the world can't help me," he said. But Sandman's spirit seemed to perk up when God led me to tell him that the book of Isaiah in the Bible calls Jesus, "Wonderful Counselor." After spending a little time together, we thanked each other for our brief bond of friendship. He was desperate for family time; hoping to connect with his children. I'm thankful that Jesus, the Light, shines in the darkness and darkness has not overcome it (John 1:5). I was greatly blessed with this brief encounter—I'm thankful for the crucial, relational ministry of Jesus. But I was shocked and deeply saddened when I found out about two months later that Sandman was shot and killed on the street. I hoped our paths would cross again, but I am thankful for the little time we shared. His friend Jan said he was a believer in Jesus—that he was gentle, kind and generous. I'm sorry I never got to see him again, but I will see him in God's presence. I miss him. I won't forget my brief acquaintance with Sandman.

Johann was an artist who lived on the street, and he liked to draw faces and told stories as he drew, even though I couldn't always follow his train of thought. I asked him, "If I just scribble something, can you turn it into a drawing?" He nodded, so I made a small scribble on the paper. He started sketching over it, and it looked just like Mary, the Mother of Jesus holding the baby Jesus. I showed it to another homeless man, and he agreed. Then Johann kept working on it and all of the sudden Mary and the baby Jesus together became a single face, which he named "Logan." Johann looked up at me and we both broke into side-splitting laughter—the first time in four years I ever saw him laugh. What a double blessing of relational joy from Jesus!

God helped me get to know and love the poor and homeless. Many of them had street names, street handles, or call signs. A few of these include Spiderman, Candy, Bear, Wolf, Rooster, Giovanne, Chains, Brandy, Toughy, Peaches, Kickback, Elbow, Stitch, Stretch, Slugbug, and Termite! One day I was shocked as I got to know Elijah, who was quiet, reserved, very kind and relational. He shared with me that he used to be addicted to hand sanitizer. But now he was a street preacher and attended Church regularly, although he still struggles with burdens from the past.

I met a very bright young street person, Janice, a recovering heroin addict who stopped "cold turkey." God allowed us to have a warm conversation. Although she did not embrace Jesus as her Savior at that time, she was kind enough to receive God's Word through a gospel handout. The following is a short excerpt from a homeless poem she wrote entitled "Front Door": "The sky is my roof; The ground is my bed; My bedroom is wherever I lay my head..."

When Allan showed me the scars on his wrist, I was stunned. He had severely cut himself in an attempt to take his life. His suicide attempt came after he planned to install safety glass for a customer, but the owner wanted him to substitute regular glass and charge the premium for safety glass. This was so repugnant to Allan; he didn't know how to handle it other than to try to kill himself. As Christ's ambassadors (2 Corinthians 5:20), we are called to love, minister and serve the poor and oppressed, even when it is "untidy, mostly unresolved and messy," as Barb Roberts, our Church Caring Ministry Director described it. Too often my life seems untidy, unresolved and messy, and God knows that it is. Ryan Taylor, who ministers to the homeless, told me he was doing well despite the normal bumps, bruises, and annoyances, which he said was just part of the big picture. I wish I had his attitude about the little frustrations in life! John 16:33 states, "I have told you these things, so that in me you may have peace. In this world you will have trouble. But take heart! I have overcome the world." Oswald Chambers stated, "The typical view of the Christian life is that it means being delivered from all adversity. But it actually means being delivered in adversity, which is something very different."

I asked a street person when it was cold, "Are you staying warm?" He looked at me cynically and asked, "Are *you* staying warm?" To help me "break the ice" with another person who was applying lotion to both legs, I asked, "You putt'n on lotion?" He sharply responded, "What's it look like!" These two brief conversations help me understand better that I often try to minister under my own strength, not trusting God to work through me. He needs to always keep me humble and grounded in Him, as I learn to love the poor and hang with the homeless, enabling me to be a better witness for Christ. Their *love* humbles me. And sometimes their *behavior* humbles me—when I watched a man slam the bathroom door, I saw my own spurts of anger. And when another man got upset with me if I ask him detailed questions about his high-tech drones or stun guns, he impatiently stated, "It doesn't matter," I heard my own sharp remarks of impatience. I still harbor those sinful character flaws, especially when I don't trust in God, and that directly undermines my testimony for Jesus.

As God connected me with a young homeless man, I thought about where he might have grown up. I asked, "Where's home for you?" He lowered his head and looked down at the table. Then he looked back up at me with a soft, gentle smile on his face, shaking his head, "I don't know." As we talked about Jesus, sadly he identified himself as being more aligned with "cults." I was thankful that we made a strong connection; he seemed like a kind young man. I hope Jesus will rescue him. Similarly, I asked a young man who lived with his mother, about his upcoming trip to Florida, where he planned to spend some time with extended family. I thought he would get to see his dad. When it seemed clear that he wouldn't, I asked him, "Where's your Dad?" He briefly lowered his head, then looked back up at me, smiled sadly and said, "I don't know." On a different day, I asked my homeless friend Nick if he was a believer in Jesus. He said, "Most of the time." When I asked what he meant, he said, "When I'm not drinking!" It's often hard for me to relate to these life stories. But Jesus knows them, and He understands rejection and suffering more than anyone.

George, my street friend and survival expert who lives in a camouflage tent, vehemently disliked me for about three years, making my life extremely difficult. He made it clear that he didn't want to see me and wished I would just go away. I dreaded hanging in that area, knowing that he would embarrass or insult me if I saw him. But over time I realized Jesus was doing a new thing. He seemed to be reconciling our relationship. Jesus brought healing to the point where we enjoyed each other's company, helping us draw nearer to Him and closer to one another. Jesus is *the healer of our hearts—the mender of our souls.*

[Song Credit: *The Healer of My Heart*—The Sisters]. George told me how he once picked up a flat, overnight express shipping box, assembled it so it looked like it had something in it, then biked to a national drag racing meet. Arriving at the gate, George told them he had parts that urgently needed delivery to a racing team and asked them to show him how to get to the "pits." They cleared him through the gate to the pits, giving him free entry into the national event! Even though I loved connecting with him, sadly one day he told me, "I wanted my Dad to die. He was not a nice person. We went to his funeral to make sure he was dead. He's dead now and that's good. Life sucks."

Sharing a brief backstory at this point seems appropriate, an example of how I suffered the physical consequences of my personal pride, a precursor for sharing something far worse. The Zamboni just finished freshening the ice, as my wife and I were enjoying an ice-skating date together. I was skating beyond my skill level as I tried to "show off" to her with my blazing speed. I started to lose control as I approached the rink wall. Next thing I knew, I cried out in agonizing pain, screaming for help. Through God's grace, a fireman was on the ice and immediately stabilized my arm. When the paramedics arrived, they took over tending to my injuries. I heard one of them say, "It's broken." The other paramedic stared sympathetically into my face, trying to comfort me. She had a beautiful smile with kind eyes, which was helpful in the moment. Because the Zamboni just came off the ice, there were still some water puddles where I "crashed and burned!" My old, beloved grayish green goose down parka had to be cut off by the paramedics. Now the disaster scene consisted of blood from an eye wound, along with water and feathers. The fall resulted in a dangerous compound spiral fracture of my arm, which could have easily resulted in nerve damage from bone fragments, if not for that fireman's intervention. God blessed me with a great orthopedic surgeon, who had his sub-specialty fellowship in trauma medicine. He stepped in when the other expected surgeon was previously scheduled. I was so thankful. He did a wonderful job, as depicted by the X-ray, revealing a 12-inch plate and 16 screws. Days later in his office, he thanked me for the gospel handout.

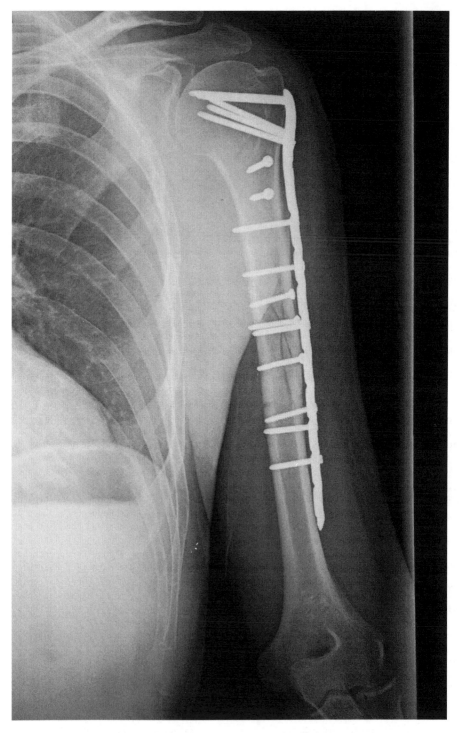

My X-ray after the compound spiral fracture
and surgery, resulting from pride.

As I recovered in the hospital a few days later, the same gorgeous paramedic, who provided comfort at the scene, approached in the hallway as I walked with assistance. When she recognized me, she said, "Hey, there's the skater!" I didn't appreciate her sense of humor at the time. I didn't go back to the ice arena for a long time, and I never skated again!

In a somewhat similar development, my wife Barbie's caregiver invited us to join their family for worship one Sunday in their Ethiopian Evangelical Church. We immensely enjoyed the visiting pastor. He told an amazing story of how God desires that we live lives of simplicity and humility. He told the Bible story of Judas Escariot, who betrayed Jesus, and who was from the tribe of Judah, a proud and rebellious tribe. But the other eleven disciples were simple and humble Galileans. Was I Listening? Was I listening to God when I agreed to join the Ethiopian Pastor and his team, which was late in the planning stages? This two-week mission trip would dedicate three Churches in a small community where the shepherds worship nightly in tiny desert chapels.

I remember the Pastor calling to tell me to please listen to his heart as he told me he felt like I was being too rushed to prepare for the trip, and the fact that it would entail a 17-hour flight. Without praying about this, and respecting his spiritual authority, I responded quickly and arrogantly, "A 17-hour flight is nothing to me—I've taken many of these flights before." Again, was I listening to God? Probably not. Did I pray about it? No. Was I suffering from personal pride again? Yes. I longed for Ethiopia, to see the birthplace of my two adopted grandchildren. The Pastor had a picture hanging in his office of when he was a young shepherd herding flocks of goats and sheep. He never thought he would become a shepherd of people. I grew to love those shepherds as I heard stories about them. I would stare at that picture of the desert chapel, as well as a beautiful painting of a small desert chapel, which hung in our Church. I longed to be with those shepherds and pray with them. I wasn't listening to God, and I didn't understand how He was working—I got in the way of His ministry. I was deeply disappointed as I applied for a refund from my cancelled mission trip. It would have been disastrous for my wife if I were away as she had three back-to-back colon surgeries.

What I haven't told you yet is that not only did these two stories demonstrate how physically destructive my natural, *personal* pride can be, but the story that follows is worse—the story of my crippling *spiritual* pride, that led to two punishing corrections from God. In spite of my pride, I hope God molds me into a loving, heart soft servant—growing me, allowing and teaching me to love and serve the poor and hang with the homeless. Director Ryan Taylor spoke of the community of love among the poorest members of society whom he was observing. John Hicks responded to my question about this love observed. He said, "God is why there's love." Yet ironically, the homeless ministry also became the place where my deeply embedded, besetting *sinsick soul* [Song Credit: *There Is A Balm In Gilead*] bubbled up to the surface. I know Jesus is alive in me because I encounter Him often in unexpected ways, most often joyfully comfortable and pleasing—but sometimes not. The consequences of me being easily ensnared and entangled in sin led to God's double correction, requiring His "I-beam" [Credit: Author Ruth Lycke] to my temple, not just His 2 X 4! One day I walked into the coffeehouse with a bag of food. I remember seeing out of the corner of my eye an attractive young lady, who clearly appeared to be a new volunteer, and she happened to be looking at me as I entered. I briefly smiled at her, but at that moment my pride overcame me. I knew, that she knew, that I was serving the poor, doing good works for God. Just minutes later I walked into a heated argument between two street people. Anger overtook me and I screamed at them to stop. Then one of them screamed back at me, "Are you a Christian? Christians sin!" I was quick to anger and gave them no grace, as Jesus gave me. I felt horrible over my actions, thinking I was compromising the ministry. This seemed to be the beginning of God's correction in this setting. He convicted me of guilt regarding my sin of anger, judgement, and lack of love, grace and forgiveness. This helped convict me that if I'm not forgiving people almost every day when they sin against me, as God forgives me for my sins, it often means I am harboring hardness in my heart.

During this time, I also found myself taking more of an interest in hanging out with the attractive female volunteers, instead of hanging with the homeless. This came to light when a homeless woman snuck up behind me and screamed directly into my ear, startling me. Now with a painful ringing in my ear, I was angry and confused as to why she would do this. Then, in my spirit, I understood that God was correcting me. Pastor Gary Moore, in the *Chaplain's Corner*, stated that the Hebrew word for *correction* (shebet) in Job 37:13 [NKJV], literally means "a stick." [e.g., to punish] God's double correction reminded me of what one Pastor said when God seemed to speak inaudibly to him over an ongoing sinful temptation, "If you use or abuse someone I brought to you to be a blessing, you will be in trouble with me."

I deluded myself into believing that there were no consequences for my sinful behavior. But I needed to do what author Paul David Tripp stated, "Use every means available to fight the delusion that what you choose to do or say doesn't make any difference." (*Forever*, p. 63 stated in the context of the [sinful] "dark side of forever.") As a result, God humbled me. I wondered if He could forgive me (The difference between knowing and feeling). God resists the proud but gives grace to the humble—I needed God's forgiving grace in my time of need. After a Bible study lesson and subsequent conversation with Pastor Joe Lloyd, he explained scripture and helped me understand that God's grace truly was greater than my sin (Romans 5:20). Author Timothy Keller helped show me why my false understanding of saving faith in this situation was devastating to me. (*Romans 1-7 For You*, p. 99) I was downcast in my soul, felt rejection, and believed Satan's lie that I was no longer wanted or needed at the ministry. I didn't expect to have a spiritual crisis of faith at age 73. I didn't feel theological—I just felt alone, guilty, in pain and ashamed, filled with regret, empty, and broken. But God rescued me from the pit, provided for me and gave me grace to help me in my time of need (Hebrews 4:16). I'm thankful for God's double correction, because sin when fully grown leads to death. The love of Jesus restored my soul, renewed a steadfast spirit within me, and granted me a willing spirit to sustain me. God gave me living hope in His living Word, Jesus Christ, so I can press on proclaiming the gospel of peace.

I'm sure I was not fully prayed up as I neared the coffeehouse in my car on those two occasions of God's double correction in my life. Now when I leave home to hang with the homeless and love the poor, I am very intentional about covering myself with God's protective prayer. Under the authority of Jesus, I ask God to provide "Holy Ground" in and around the coffee house, especially since several of these people have died from unnatural causes. I pray harder before I arrive—I don't ever want to be corrected by God like that again. An example of how I prayerfully prepare whenever I approach the coffeehouse is, "Heavenly Father, Jesus Christ, Holy Spirit, discipline me, punish me if necessary, teach me to do your will, show me any offensive way within me. Fill me with your Holy Spirit, indwell me with your Holy Spirit, empower me with your Holy Spirit, baptize me with your Holy Spirit. Help me and heal me, lead me and control me, guide me and counsel me. Reach out with your mighty hand and out-stretched arm, place your hedge of protection over me, send an angel ahead of me, protect my heart from the Evil One, protect me physically. I don't know what to do but my eyes are on you. Tell me where to go and what to do. Tell me what I've been assigned to do. Not my will but Thy will shall be done. He must become greater; I must become less. Let your words be my words. Speak Lord for your servant is listening. I will do everything you want me to do.' Jesus said, 'Apart from me, you can do nothing.' 'Heavenly Father, Jesus Christ, Holy Spirit, I raise holy hands to you. I claim victory as an overcomer in Christ. I claim freedom from bondage. Heavenly Father, show me where you are working so I can see your work and do your work in like manner. Help me to do what is in your heart and mind."

> Heavenly Father, show me where you are working so I can see your work and do your work in like manner. Help me to do what is in your heart and mind.
> —paraphrased from John 5:19, 20 and 1 Samuel 2:35

Sometimes I continue praying something like, "Trust in the Lord with all your heart and lean not on your own understanding. In all your ways acknowledge Him and He will make your paths straight. I put on the full armor of God. Create in me a pure heart, O God, and renew a steadfast spirit within me. Grant me a willing spirit to sustain me." Through God's power, I ask Him to resist, rebuke, cast out, and bind up the devil, Satan, his demons and evil angels so they will flee—doomed to eternal condemnation in the lake of fiery Hell.

It is uplifting in my spirit as I pray and put on the full armor of God. With the gospel of peace, I slowly and softly stretch out the word *peace* so it sounds like *peeeeeacccce*, just because for me it mysteriously helps slow and settle my mind down and quiets my heart and spirit toward the deeper things of God (1 Corinthians 2:10).

Jesus Christ holds everything together (Colossians 1:16, 17), just as in like manner, I am minded of what is sometimes called a "Jesus nut" on helicopters, which also "holds everything together." If I try to hang with the homeless, love the poor and proclaim the gospel without God's help, my spiritual life often becomes ineffective and tends to fall apart—reminding me of when Jesus said, "Apart from me you can do nothing." The term "Jesus nut," refers to the main rotor retaining nut that holds the main rotor to the mast on helicopters and represents a potential single point of failure that would have catastrophic consequences. While on a business trip, I was waiting for my airline flight, with some time before departure. I walked over to police helicopter operations right by the terminal and asked the man behind the counter if he was familiar with the term "Jesus nut." He immediately responded that he was, and was kind enough to give me the old used "Jesus nut" pictured here, since it was no longer airworthy.

"Jesus nut" example from a helicopter.

In the Bible God warns us to be ready, be watching, and throw off sin that so easily entangles us (Hebrews 12:1). I not only need to avoid sin, but I need to watch my patterns of behavior and avoid things that can lead to sin. I have been vulnerable in relationships with female friendships that can lead to an unhealthy attraction (1 John 2:16—lust of the flesh and eyes). It doesn't help me when an attractive woman dresses provocatively. It is distracting and attention getting. I have to fight the temptation to dwell instead of fleeing. Often, I say to myself, "Dave, don't even look." As one pastor said, "The first look is free. The second look will cost you!" Lust and idol worship can come in many forms. I can spot a Rosso Corsa Ferrari F-430 F1 coupe from a distance on one side and a voluptuous woman on the other. Lord, help me keep my eyes straight ahead (Proverbs 4:25), and my heart pure (Psalm 51:10). In Proverbs, Solomon clearly spelled out the importance of moral purity, and the hazards of moral impurity (Credit: Dr. David Jeremiah) While hanging with the homeless, I asked Robin, the shift lead, if she would show Myron, a first time visitor at the homeless ministry, pictures of her oil paintings. Robin pulled out her cell phone, found the pictures, and handed Myron the phone. So Myron looked through all her work, but stopped at some paintings Robin did when practicing the nude female form. We were humorously shocked and surprised. But then I quickly recognized the fine line—high risk occupation in which we were engaged; especially for someone living on the street, struggling with addictions. For guys, it can turn from art appreciation into sinful lust in a heartbeat! We can so easily become entangled, distracted and ensnared in sinful pleasure, particularly with suggestive graphics. I am amazed at the fact that God can use even a sinner like me to do His work. C.S. Lewis had excellent insight, in his book *Surprised By Joy*, p. 170 stating, "I sometimes wonder whether all pleasures are not substitutes for Joy."

> "I sometimes wonder whether all pleasures are not substitutes for Joy."
> —C.S. Lewis

chapter 10

Soul Winner's Joy

The greatest way God manifested the comforting
Peace of Christ in me was through the time of my eternal salvation,
described in the first chapter of this book. One of the greatest and
most joyfully thrilling manifestations of God's *Presence* was through mysterious
deep, sacred soul winner's joy—the indescribable, infinitely majestic cause/effect
relationship between obediently proclaiming the gospel, even in persecution and
suffering, and the resultant intensified, blessedness of unfolding "Jesus Joy."
Jesus *saved* my life, and proclaiming Jesus *changed* my life.

My wife, Barbie, and I pray for the salvation of many of her caregivers.
But sometimes we wonder what God is doing when we are unable to see Him
working in their lives. One day the Holy Spirit seemed to prompt me to make
a risky statement. I said to Barbie's caregiver, Vivian,
"You seem like a really sweet sinner!" She didn't even
revolt, as it was humbly received, and upon which she
agreed. Thankfully, I survived that one! When Barbie
and I were on vacation by the ocean visiting friends, we
met a very nice young man named Jonathan, a lifeguard
at the hotel. We enjoyed a brief friendship together

*Jesus saved
my life, and
proclaiming
Jesus changed
my life.*

and had a few spiritual conversations over several days. He shared about his
upbringing on an island, and how he was passionate about surfing. Then the
time came for us to leave, but I did not want to part ways without giving him the

gospel. On top of a huge water slide, I shared scripture and my testimony with him. I asked Jonathan where he would spend eternity, because he told me he was fearful he would die riding giant pipeline waves. "Honestly, I'm not sure," he responded. My wife and I, along with our friends, tried to stay in touch with him. The last we heard; he was going back to live on the island where he grew up. I have often prayed for his salvation.

Whether on the trail, in a grocery store or doctor's office—I never know where, when, or how the Holy Spirit is going to bless me with "Jesus joy," as I proclaim the gospel. I was just about to leave the gas station one afternoon after filling up my car, when an elderly lady walked up to me and asked if I could help loosen the gas cap on her car. I quickly parked, grabbed a gospel handout, helped her and gave her the good news. Even though I only had about 10-15 seconds with her, she kindly received God's Word. Another example was Cory at the grocery store cash register—he wore a baseball cap with a radically curbed bill, and the hat was pulled down covering much of his face and eyes. He seemed detached in his demeanor. As I completed checking out, I offered the gospel handout to him; then he did something unexpected. He stared at the graphic for several seconds, then looked into my eyes for several seconds and in great sincerity of heart said, "Thank you!" What a great joy to see the Word of God received with a heartfelt welcome and great gratitude. Sometimes the blessing is mysterious and perplexing, driving me to pray—a man named Dexter reached out for help as I approached the store he was standing near. He claimed to be hungry and initially asked for food. After about a 15-minute strange sharing encounter both outside and inside the store, I didn't know if he truly needed help, was on drugs, or perhaps a drug dealer—his story was so obscure and disjointed. I wished I had prayed for discernment before I got out of my car. As God brings people across my path, I don't know if they *know* Jesus, are seeking Him with all their heart, or just desperately seeking Jesus even if they don't know it—We all need Jesus.

My airline flight was in the boarding process as I sat down in my seat and prayed that I would be able to proclaim the gospel to someone. Although the man on my right was from a different nation and culture, I thought it might be him, but he was not communicative. As I watched people continue boarding, I saw a tall, young handsome man wearing beach shorts, curly bleached blond hair, sunglasses on top of his head looking very "cool" and carefree. I prayed, "God, please don't let it be him."

But God, as usual, had other plans, which became clear when the "cool" young man sat down in the empty seat on my left. I introduced myself and found out his name was Mike. He spoke about his precision carpentry work on luxury homes in the mountains and of the wealthy people who owned numerous homes in different locations. Then he told me about a man who came to inspect his work on an expensive bay window in his fancy vacation home. It was not perfect in his eyes, so he ordered Mike to rip

I prayed, "God, please don't let it be him."

it all out and start over—then he left! This cost the owner large sums of money, but it didn't appear to be an issue. Mike explained to me that this is not unusual. Through the course of the flight, I went through the plan of salvation with him, using a gospel handout. After a long, friendly conversation, Mike dedicated (or rededicated) his life to Christ—opening his heart to the gospel of peace. While Mike isn't who I would have picked, he is the one God picked for me to proclaim His Word, and how great was my joy knowing that we will enjoy God for all eternity and that I was allowed to play a small part in making that happen.

Exodus 15:2 states, "The Lord is my strength and my defense; He has become my salvation. He is my God, and I will praise Him, my father's God, and I will exalt Him." God is my strength to boldly *proclaim* the gospel, and salvation is only *through* the gospel. At the Post Office one day I was waiting in line, very tired, holding three packages, and I did not feel like proclaiming the gospel. I told God, "I can't do it." But I promised Him I would tell the good news of Jesus if He helped me—He did, so I did! He allowed me to speak with the lady in front of me, whose name was Annette. I clumsily offered her a gospel handout to give to her daughter, to whom she was sending a care package at college. Then, I noticed that it was already wrapped and addressed. Annette said, "I need that," and kept it for herself. We had a delightful chat, which I was not expecting. She drew near to God's living Word of eternal life. I praised God in my heart for allowing me to be part of His plan to bring hope and life—what indescribable joy. On another occasion at the Post Office, I stood in line behind a woman of a different nationality. As far as I could see, there was no way I could connect with her, so I assumed God was not going to use me that day. But the God who called into being that which did not exist (Romans 4:17) made a way where there was no way. I initiated a greeting on faith, and the lady named Audrey and I were able to speak as we waited in line. She kindly received a gospel handout. As I left the Post Office, I saw her reading God's Word in the handout at the counter as she waited for her package to be processed. And then on another occasion at the Post Office, a woman named Susi was preparing several large packages on the counter, behind which were postal forms displayed in a slotted rack. She allowed me get a certified mail form behind her packages. I thanked her for her kindness and gave her a gospel handout which she was kind enough to receive with thankfulness. Then she said, "That's what I want my legacy to be...my kindness."

Even if people are not believers, they often receive God's word wholeheartedly. But there are times when they do not, typically responding with, "I'm OK," or "I'm good!" I am often doubly blessed when a *believer* accepts the gospel handout. Sometimes they start to hand it back to me. I often respond with, "Let me ask you a question. Do you think you know anybody who might be low on hope, and needs encouragement?" They almost always say "Yes," or "Sure, I know somebody." And they quickly take it back. What a joy it brings knowing that God is at work spreading His love and salvation, and that I was privileged to play a part in His divine plan.

The gospel is not just for family and friends, but for everyone everywhere.

I was reminded of how important it is to be spiritually ready, watching and prepared as the Holy Spirit leads, to give a defense and proclaim the gospel. On the hiking trail near my home, I had not yet offered the gospel handout to anyone, on this particular day, even though I had them in my pocket, ready to retrieve. Then just as I headed home, I arrived at the bridge where a lady named Kate watched her children play near the small stream. It was a very brief encounter with a short greeting and comment about the approaching snowstorm. I gave her a gospel handout, which she kindly received, and thanked me for the good news.

If we don't proclaim the gospel when God opens a door of ministry, it comes at great opportunity cost. The gospel is not just for family and friends, but for everyone, just as Jesus died for everyone.

Perhaps one way to get a faint glimpse of the magnitude of God's overarching connection between proclaiming the gospel and the resulting joy of the proclaimer is through two excerpts from the book of James. In chapter 1, verses 1-4 James wrote, "Consider it pure joy, my brothers and sisters, whenever you face trials of many kinds, because you know that the testing of your faith produces perseverance. Let perseverance finish its work so that you may be mature and complete, not lacking anything." And later in the same chapter, there is an important distinction between *doing* versus just *hearing* the Word, in verses 22-25, "Do not merely listen to the word, and so deceive yourselves. Do what it says. Anyone who listens to the word but does not do what it says is like someone who looks at his face in a mirror and, after looking at himself, goes away and immediately forgets what he looks like. But whoever looks intently into the perfect law that gives freedom and continues in it—not forgetting what they have heard but doing it—they will be blessed in what they do." That may be one of the reasons Robert E. Coleman spoke of being "Supremely Soul Winning" in *The Master Plan of Evangelism*, P. 73, and why evangelist Bill Fay refers to *not* proclaiming the gospel as "The sin of silence." Andrew, an evangelist in a hostile country, was filled with grace, even in persecution for his faith, when he stated, "We are wasting our time if we don't learn how to preach the gospel." (*Voice of the Martyrs* (VOM) January 2019, page 9)

"We are wasting our time if we don't learn how to preach the gospel."
—Andrew

When God blesses us with His joy as we proclaim the gospel, it is not just joy for joy's sake—but out of His forgiving grace He allows us the great honor and privilege to know, love, serve and obey Him—He blesses us with joy afterwards, as we proclaim the gospel of peace through the love of Christ Jesus. Perhaps the joy comes from feeling His presence more deeply. Maybe that is one reason God placed joy second, immediately following love, on the list of the fruit of the Spirit

(Galatians 5:22). I need to keep proclaiming the gospel, expecting to *get* nothing, but *receiving* everything.

James 2:17 states in part, "...faith by itself, if it is not accompanied by action, is dead." Whether I like it or not, I live in a cosmic, spiritual war zone—I am engaged, along with fellow believers, in the *"war of all wars."* [author of this term unknown] Our wonderful friend, Viva, a radiant young believer in a distant land, new in her faith, clandestinely met with her spiritual brothers and sisters in the back of a restaurant. One day the *bluecoats* took their names and addresses and informed them that they could not do this anymore. God opened a door for my wife Barbie to encourage her, especially since Viva may have to pay a high price for her faith in Christ in a hostile, highly restricted country closed to the gospel. "May the courage of our persecuted brothers and sisters inspire you to be a bold witness for Christ!" *The Voice of the Martyrs* (VOM)

"May the courage of our persecuted brothers and sisters inspire you to be a bold witness for Christ!" —The Voice of the Martyrs

Rev. John Fox quoted an eyewitness to 70 Christians in the year 1560 having their throats cut, stating, "Another thing I must mention, the patience with which they met death: they seemed all resignation and piety, fervently praying to God and cheerfully encountering their fate." (*Fox's Book of Martyr's* p. 192)

Persecution toward me because of my trust in Jesus has been minimal. At work I was once disparagingly called "Reverend [last name omitted]" by a colleague at work with a PhD in education, and mockingly labeled "Jesus freak" by another. I have sometimes been ridiculed, challenged, rebuked and laughed at when proclaiming my faith in Jesus. I've had a few things thrown at me, but mostly overt and covert words from mild to wild, meant to ostracize, distance, detach, and insult—yet nobody has ever been able to steal my joy in Jesus.

While I served overseas, persecution was more intense at times. During the first few weeks my wife, Barbie, and I served in a Mideastern country, I was confused and became depressed from the injustice I saw all around. Our lives wove back and forth through contested borders, walls of separation, disputed fences, barriers and barricades, always in the presence of guns. Then one day we traveled with two missionaries who introduced us to Aaron, a believer with a background in Islam who evangelized Muslims. Aaron greatly suffered as he served the Lord—he was persecuted for his faith and his life was often threatened, sometimes with words on the telephone, "You're just a bullet away." When in a dimly lit underground office, I looked into his face and saw both the deep agony of Christ, and the great love of Jesus. In that precise moment God instantly healed me of depression. Aaron's deep joy, in spite of intense persecution, helped me better understand that true justice is only through Jesus. Even though most people we met tended to take sides in this spiritual battle for justice, Barbie and I were joyfully blessed to meet a few Christians who did not take sides but prayed for the salvation of all.

Neither my wife nor I suffered to the extent that Aaron did. Over time Barbie and I had rocks and sticks thrown at us; she was shot with a BB gun, and I was kicked hard many times by a young boy in a refugee camp. We were held at gunpoint twice in one hour by two politically opposed factions in the middle of the night on the way to the airport. On another occasion we had a gun pointed at us, while commanded to stop approaching. We feared for our lives in a few other instances. Would we get shot driving late at night along the border where another person had just been ambushed and killed? On

> Aaron's deep joy, in spite of intense persecution, helped me better understand that true justice is only through Jesus.

another day we thought, "Please don't stone us to death," after we got lost in the city and many angry ultra-orthodox believers glared at us for driving on a "no driving street," on a religious holiday. But this light persecution was virtually nothing compared to true Christian martyrs (witnesses), evangelists and pastors whose lives are on the line in countries closed to the gospel. God makes clear in His Holy Word the inexpressible and glorious *joy of obedience* (Credit: Cole Richards—VOM), as we preach the gospel, even in suffering (e.g., 1 Peter 1 and Matthew 5). Even when the journey of proclaiming the gospel is painstaking, God's mysterious joy never leaves me.

Once when I prayed for persecuted Christians, it took me three hours to write three sentences to a pastor whose life was on the line for his faith in Jesus. These pastors are willing to sacrifice their lives, and often do, for the salvation of lives that are spiritually lost and destined for eternal condemnation in the Lake of Fire (Romans 5:8, 5:12). If we know and love Jesus as our Savior, shouldn't we be willing, as the Holy Spirit leads, to do our part, and do what Jesus commands in Mark 16:15, "...preach the gospel to all creation?" My struggle to write just a few sentences to a pastor risking everything for Christ helped convict me to do my part in God's kingdom plan, as the Holy Spirit leads.

In 1989 our family visited the Berlin wall just a couple months before it was torn down. Many years later I saw a picture of a van outfitted with secret compartments for smuggling Bibles into East Germany during that same time, the late 1980's. God's Holy Word shall go forth (Isaiah 2:3), it shall not return void or empty (Isaiah 55:11), and the gates of hell shall not prevail against God's Church (Matthew 16:17-19). The funny thing about those gates is that they don't move. So, in order for the Church to prevail against them, the Church must do its part and actually go out to spread the gospel. While serving in the Mideast in 2009, along with cleaning toilets, laundry, and meal preparation, one of my jobs was to smuggle believers across borders every Sunday to worship in the Church from which they had been displaced. Later, when we departed the country, the last thing we were told at the airport was, "You'll be restricted." Perhaps this was because for months we served the body of Christ on the "wrong side" of the border and crossed over nearly one hundred times, having been checked and queried at guard posts, verified in border guard's computers, and probably categorized as a "collaborator" with the "enemy," who ironically were Christians. I'm thankful for our wonderful missionary friend, Terry Madison, who was on the Project Pearl team in 1981, smuggling a million Bibles into China—thankful nobody died. Christians have a long history of "Holy Smuggling" of Bibles! These include *"God's Smuggler,"* (Brother Andrew) and millions of Christians who have smuggled Bibles in suitcases, clothing, parachutes, balloons, vehicles, and even donkeys trained to be without a handler.

Unfortunately, I have often been fearful and uncourageous in helping advance God's kingdom of heaven work. I remember preparing to board a plane in London many years ago, headed to a country hostile to Christianity. I had a large quantity of gospel handouts I was planning to distribute, stowed in my airplane carry-ons, so they would not be confiscated in my luggage. But I became fearful that these would be discovered by authorities prior to departure, or upon arrival (I'm sure I didn't stop and pray about my fear). So just minutes before getting in line for departure, I began to progressively throw quantities of them into the trash can near the boarding gate, hoping nobody would become suspicious. Later, while in that country, I deeply regretted not having enough courage to keep them for distribution, because the owner of a Bible bookstore wanted a large quantity, which was a great joy to me. Months later, I shipped gospel handouts back into the country at great expense, difficulty, time, frustration and hassles with customs. I should have trusted God—faith over fear. I have had limited impact in countries where evangelism is illegal. Yet God has blessed me with underlying joy in these gospel encounters, even after I found out there was a $10,000 reward to report any case of evangelism. Pastor Richard Wurmbrand (VOM) once told a journalist, "There is no work without risk. It is a much greater risk to appear before God with the guilt of having allowed one-third of the world to perish without the knowledge of Jesus Christ. So, we take all these risks, though we are very cautious."

I have been inspired by many bold, courageous believers who take risks to proclaim the gospel, the greatest message in the history of the universe. These include imprisoned Pastors, many of whom you may well know. A few of these joyful believers include Juvi, who proclaims the gospel with fellow hotel employees and guests; Donnette, a cashier, who boldly hands gospel handouts to customers at the grocery store checkout counter; and Aunty Kanai's *Church on the Road*, who makes and sells marinade made with Aloha and Prayer [business as mission] with the purpose to proclaim Jesus. There is also Victorious, a warehouse club employee who proclaims the gospel with customers as she works.

Perhaps you have heard believers joke about "Beach evangelism," when they are on a tropical island family vacation. My wife Barbie and I were unexpectedly and mysteriously blessed on a trip to Hawaii where God showed us many wonderful ways in which He was working. We met Sheri, a Christian producer/agent, and Derick, whom she sponsors. Derick is a blind professional surfer who competed in the world surfing championships on the North Shore of Oahu. Since he was blind, Barbie asked him how he was able to surf. He responded, "God shows me!"

Derick has a joyful heart! The following related excerpt is from Oswald Chambers, *My Utmost for His Highest*, p. 67, "The surf that distresses the

Derick responded, "God shows me!"

ordinary swimmer produces in the surf-rider the super-joy of going clean through it. Apply that to our own circumstances, these very things—tribulation, distress, persecution, produce in us the super-joy; they are not things to fight. We are more than conquerors through Him *in* all these things, not in spite of them, but in the midst of them. The saint never knows the joy of the Lord in spite of tribulation, but *because* of it— 'I am exceedingly joyful in all our tribulation,' says Paul."

One day I left a store where three women received gospel handouts. While driving to another store, I felt defeated, like I failed because I was not able to proclaim God's Holy Word with any men that day. I was very tired and felt downcast in my spirit. I didn't think there was any chance I would give a gospel handout to a man that day. I got out of the car and walked toward the store, low on hope and desperately in need of God's grace. Near the store front, an elderly man opened the door for me. "Thank you, that's really nice of you," I said. "Yea, kinder than usual." "I'll bet you're a really kind man." "Yea, how much money you got!" "I've got the greatest news in the world," and I offered him a gospel handout, which he was kind enough to receive. Daryl stared at it. He looked at me. Then he reached out and shook my hand. I was filled with the joy of God's sovereignty. As I shopped around the store, I kept hoping our paths would cross again. I called him by name later in the store, with a question about where I could find something, for which he was very helpful, almost like we were old friends. Thank you, Lord, for your grace in time of need. I walked slowly back to the car, pondering what God just did for me; and for Daryl whom He loves and for whom Jesus died. I sat in the car for a few minutes; then sadly confessed, "Sorry Lord I gave up on you." Time after time God demonstrates to me this excerpt from Ephesians 3, "...to grasp how wide and long and high and deep is the love of Christ, and to know this love that surpasses knowledge—that you may be filled to the measure of all the fullness of God."

As I continued my painstaking journey toward soul winner's joy, I became more curious about what some of my believing friends experience—those whom I know give the gift of the gospel. I asked them how they experience joy when proclaiming Jesus, and to what they attribute that joy. Cheryl Leonhardt said, "Well done, good and faithful servant—we are communing with God. We are in the center of His will." Pastor Ruben Rodriguez said, "Recall—we recall the joy that we experienced when we accepted Christ." Erik Witt said, "It is my greatest joy; nothing like it; proclaiming the best news of all time. It is my greatest desire. No greater feeling regardless of whether you are planting, watering or harvesting." Galen Malenke, a great user of gospel handouts who often ministers to those in jail, stated, "There's no greater joy than to see somebody use my feeble words to make a decision that affects them for eternity. For some unknown reason, I always feel like I'm going into jail for the first time. I identify with Paul when he said his weakness was his greatest strength. I guess God wants me to be 100% dependent on Him. Availability, not ability, applies to me." Alison Kreeger stated, "What drew my coworker to me was the uncommon joy of Christ in me." G. Paul Miller encouraged me when he said, "Building a genuine relationship of trust, naturally leads to a spiritual conversation. They see a difference in my life. They are asking...in a sincere friendship..." Reggie said, "When I share the gospel, I feel like I'm serving my purpose—remain faithful to God." Bob Emeott asked, "How can you not smile when you think about the gospel?" Scott Brennan, J.D., friend and Chaplain volunteer for an alternative high school said, "It's not that my wife nor I are afraid to work for the Lord, but isn't it amazing and joyful when all you have to do is explain how it works to lost souls, and then watch as the Lord himself does all the work in ushering people into His kingdom." Scott and his wife, Louise, proclaim the gospel with kids who have committed a crime or have no home life. They pray, trusting God for kids to give their life to Christ—then disciple those kids through ongoing Church services and Bible study. University Professor Charles E. (Chuck) King J.D., who led me to Christ in 1980, is a skilled apologist. He asked great spiritual questions, and answered the tough ones, like an unbeliever in China who once asked him, "How can you believe in a God who allows little children to die?" [which opened up a conversation] Chuck enjoyed the process of proclaiming the gospel, discipling and fellowship—even when he doesn't see the results. As he mentored young people, he often asked questions about "life direction." To new believers he may ask something like, "What are you going to do with this faith you've accepted?" Because Chuck is a humble man, his wife, Jeanene shared with me, "He has a quiet witness, but powerful—people hunger for that." I was so blessed by their answers to my questions. Bless somebody today with Jesus, the ultimate blessing from Genesis 12:3, 4. Proclaiming Him, and the blessing of "Jesus joy" go hand in hand. In reference to Galatians 2:14, Tim Keller wrote in *Galatians for You*, p. 53, "Christian living is therefore a continual realignment process—one of bringing everything in line with the truth of the gospel."

I was excited to hear my friend Bill Warner tell how he and his wife were joyfully and unexpectedly blessed through a mysterious and unlikely encounter with the IRS. During the course of a grueling day with no lunch, constantly grilled by the IRS agent through an intense tax audit, the Holy Spirit spontaneously worked through them. Bill said, "The Holy Spirit works through us [Christians at large] without us knowing it." At the conclusion of the day, they hugged the lady agent and said, "Thank you very much for this day." She cried. Bill described this as, "Nine hours of Christian witness without quoting scripture!" This reminded me of one of Bill's devotional quotes, "A man's steps are directed by the Lord. How can anyone understand His own way?" (Proverbs 20:24) "God places His saints where they will bring the most glory to Him, and we are totally incapable of judging where that may be." (Credit: Oswald Chambers). Bill made a joyful and profound impact on my life, for which I am deeply grateful. After my first wife, Nancy, died, he prayed for me every morning for years, around 4:30 a.m. He often signed off on his daily devotion, "It's a tough world—stay prayed up." He rose early every day and sometimes confessed to God that he was, "So dry."

[spiritually] Then God mysteriously filled him up and showed him the Biblical Word and words to use that day.

A mystery God blessed and pressed upon me, was the common thread that weaves through proclaiming the gospel and rejoicing in my heart. God's Word helped me better understand this. In 1 Thessalonians 1:6 the Bible states, "You became imitators of us and of the Lord, for you welcomed the message in the midst of severe suffering with the joy given by the Holy Spirit." And 1 Thessalonians 2:8, states "..., so we cared for you. Because we loved you so much, we were delighted to share with you not only the gospel of God but our lives as well." And King David in Psalm 51:12 wrote, "Restore to me the joy of your salvation and grant me a willing spirit, to sustain me." I was blessed by author Arthur W. Pink as he described David as, "The sweet Psalmist of Israel. Although King David was stained by sin, he had a tender conscience—a mark of true spirituality." (Paraphrased, *The Life of David*, pp. 117, 118) I'm thankful for Luke 15:7 which states, "I tell you that in the same way there will be more rejoicing in heaven over one sinner who repents than over ninety-nine righteous persons who do not need to repent."

In my curiosity to understand the correlation between proclaiming the gospel and this mysterious joy, I was led to study some Old Testament Hebrew scriptures. I found to my surprise, the meanings behind the presence of the Hebrew word for joy was often in association with direct references to distinctly Messianic prophecy (delivered, redeemed, salvation, rescued, Savior). There often was an overarching exuberant expression not implicit in other non-messianic prophecies. The following are examples of the Old Testament scriptures studied, along with the number of the Strong's Concordance Hebrew word reference: Psalm 51:12 - 8342; 71:23 - 7442; 95:1 -7321; 132:16 - 7442; Isaiah 35:1 - 1523, 10 - 8342; 44:23 - 7442; 51:11 - 8057, 8342; 52:9 - 6476, and Habakkuk 3:18 - 1523, 5937. These sometimes include, in part, to overcome, cry out, shout for joy, exaltation, exhortation of wisdom, praise, singing out, rejoicing, et. al. In New Testament Greek there is often an implied reference to Jesus in the presence of the word joy. The exuberant words for joy, such as charas (Hebrews 12:2 - Strong's Concordance Greek word reference 5479: joy, gladness, a source of joy.

from chairo; cheerfulness; i.e., Calm delight) appear less frequently, especially in some cases where the context does not include Jesus.

Everyone wants to be happy, but true happiness can only be found in obedience to God. He wants me as a bondservant, in strict training, to be wise and win souls—to save some (Proverbs 11:30, 1 Corinthians 9). What a wonderful word in Greek, *euangelistou*—an evangelist, a missionary, bearer of good tidings; from euaggelizo; a preacher of the gospel. I'm deeply grateful for the heavenly link; the correlation between proclaiming the gospel and the associated life changing soul winner's joy of Jesus. Acts 10:36 states, "You know the message God sent to the people of Israel, announcing the good news of peace through Jesus Christ, who is Lord of all." It brings to mind the legal doctrine of *res ipsa loquitur* (the thing speaks for itself). The joy of proclaiming Jesus speaks for itself! What a wonderful God-given, God-driven unmistakable mysterious correlation!

Leading up to the day of God doing a new thing in me (Isaiah 43:19), granting me mysterious deep, sacred soul winner's joy, the Holy Spirit convicted me to proclaim the gospel, sharing God's Word through gospel handouts at the NFL conference championship football game. This became a turning point in my life as a believer. There was an atmosphere of excitement and expectation as the big game drew near. On game day, after arriving by light rail and bus, I saw the enormous crowd pouring in as I approached the stadium—tailgate parties were in full swing, along with the aroma of BBQ grills and tasty burgers. The hometown sellout crowd anticipated a big win with home field advantage, and a ticket to the super bowl. But I never entered the stadium—my spiritual battlefield was outside. I wished I had asked for prayer coverage before engaging in battle. In retrospect, Matthew 18:19, 20 convicted me regarding what God will do in relation to asking, when believers are in agreement.

Initially, I began placing gospel handouts on vehicle windshields in the massive parking lot outside the stadium, watching for and dodging roving police cars monitoring the lot. I soon grew weary of the police and moved to the crowd of tailgaters who were eating, drinking, listening on their radios and watching on their TVs in the parking lot. As the game progressed, I could hear an occasional outburst of cheering, but overall, it was unusually subdued—things weren't going well. As I sought out people with whom to proclaim the good news of Jesus, I asked an inebriated tailgating partier how I could pray for him. He wanted our team to win, which despite intense emotions of the game, his prayer request seemed so spiritually shallow and hollow to me. After realizing that many of the tailgaters were under the influence of alcohol, I approached a bluecoat security guard and made the "mistake" of proclaiming God's Holy Word to him. "You can't do that here," he barked. I wasn't expecting to have my plans turned upside down. After a couple hours of frustrating efforts to proclaim Christ, I broke down in despair and resignation. I walked over to a bench, sat down, and burst into tears, crying like a baby and praying, "God, how could you allow me to be convicted by the Holy Spirit to come down here and proclaim the gospel, and then seemingly bear no good fruit that lasts?" I was brokenhearted and crushed in spirit (Psalm 34:18). When I finally got up enough energy to move on, in defeat, I started walking in the direction of the light rail/bus station to return home, spiritually wounded and feeling alone, distant from God. As I headed away from the stadium, I noticed two men approaching, and one of them carried a large sign that read, "Jesus Saves." I walked past them and continued on—for perhaps another 50 feet, then the Holy Spirit turned me around and sent me back to these two men. I told them how I proclaimed the gospel, and about my encounter with the security guard, at which time one of the men pointed toward an exit and asked, "You see that bridge over there? If you cross that bridge, they can't stop you." So, with a glimmer of hope, and a little bit of faith, I headed for that bridge, crossed over, and waited.

After the game ended and people began flowing out of the stadium, hundreds if not a few thousand angry, frustrated, disappointed and defeated fervent football fans headed directly toward me. I didn't know what was going to happen as I began to hold up gospel handouts in my hand, offering them to the fans as they passed by. I wondered if someone who was drunk would smash me in my face with his fist—but God protected me. Over a period of about an hour or more, approximately 125-175 gospel handouts containing only God's Word, were received by fans—some willingly, some reluctantly. Many welcomed my proclamation, "Jesus Loves You," some encouraged me. Many did not. I remember one man loudly asked me a spiritual question from a distance, having turned around after he walked past me. I don't remember his exact words, but I joyfully responded that I'd be happy to speak with him about it—he didn't take me up on my offer. With great joy, I will never forget the vision of sunlight breaking through the clouds and light mist, shining on the bright red gospel handout in my upheld hand, as the crowd continued passing by. As more and more people received the good news, I began to experience great and mysterious joy as never before. I was thankful when an occasional fan would affirm what I was doing, through a smile, or a "thank you." But I noticed that some fans dropped the gospel handouts containing God's Word on the ground as they continued on. When the crowd diminished, I followed in their path, picking up crushed gospel handouts, approximately 12-15, some of which I keep as reminders. They were thrown away, then trampled on in the mist, and ground into the dirt—they were crushed like Christ, reminding me of Isaiah 53:5, "But He was pierced for our transgressions, He was crushed for our iniquities; the punishment that brought us peace was on Him, and by His wounds we are healed." God delivered me through this time of proclamation and gave me victory as an overcomer in Christ—unspeakable joy. As I rode the bus back to my Mother-in-Law's house to pick up my wife after the game, I was basking in the glory of spiritual victory. But sadly, I arrogantly and unlovingly dismissed an unbeliever's rejection of God's Word on the bus ride, as I focused on speaking with the driver, who apparently was a believer. Spiritual pride followed quickly in the footsteps of victory. Notwithstanding that failure, I was so excited to get home and call my brother Pastor Bruce. I told him what God did at the football game, and asked him, "Help me understand what just happened?" He responded by saying, "That's called Soul Winner's Joy." I never heard that term before, but immediately understood in my spirit what God did in the heart of His servant—I was *Surprised by Joy* [Credit: C.S. Lewis] In my obedience, God exchanged my brokenheartedness and tears, for His mysterious, unspeakable deep, sacred soul winner's joy. Nehemiah 8:10 tells me in part, "...the joy of the Lord is your strength." I didn't expect God would fill me with desperate tears, and indescribable joy that day.

Warren W. Wiersbe in his book *Bless You,* spoke of The Joyful Benediction, p. 161, where Jude 1:24 includes a reference to "...with great joy—" Wonderfully, I was thrilled to discover that the Greek manuscript in this context (agalliasei) translates to wild joy! As you proclaim God's free grace gift of freedom in Jesus, the gospel of peace, sometimes in painstaking toil and suffering, may you be filled to overflowing with the blessing of exuberant "Jesus Joy," deep, sacred, divine Soul Winner's Joy—yes, even Wild Joy in Jesus! True freedom is found in being a bondservant of Christ. [Credit: Frank Ballesteri] The paradox of having true freedom in Christ by being His bondservant is that He frees us from loneliness, emptiness, fear, anxiety, and purposelessness. To be free from them is to be truly free indeed. (Paraphrased Credit: Pastor Alistair Begg)

Several billion people around the world are unsaved and spiritually lost, including some of those with whom God allows you and me to cross paths, every single day. They are wondering when their soul will be satisfied—when eternity set in their hearts by God will be fulfilled. Their eternal soul is worth saving. They are waiting for good news to come their way—waiting for you **They are wondering and waiting.** and for me, all together, partners in the gospel, to proclaim living hope [not a false hope] in Jesus Christ, the living Word. They are wondering and waiting.

Made in the USA
Lexington, KY
03 December 2019